D1143215

EAST SUSSEX COUNTY COUNCIL
WITHDRAWN
0 4 FEB 2022

03.
2 3 OCT
2 0

03573845

Ferries and Pleasure Steamers
A COLOUR PORTFOLIO

DAVID L. WILLIAMS and RICHARD DE KERBRECH

Ian Allan
PUBLISHING

Jubilee Queen (Previous page)

(7/1977) Chapman & Hewitt
200 passengers
98grt; 80ft (24.38m) loa x 21ft (6.40m) beam
Chapman & Hewitt Boatbuilders, Wadebridge, Cornwall
2 x oil, 2SA 6-cyl 6LX, by L. Gardner & Sons, Manchester, driving twin
screws: 300bhp

The *Jubilee Queen* was built in HM the Queen's Silver Jubilee year and hence was named in honour of that event. The photograph, taken from the Rock–Padstow Ferry, shows her in August 1977, a month after she entered service, while on an excursion in the River Camel Estuary. At the end of that season her bridge parapet and dodger were raised so that she could be steered from a monkey island atop the bridge. In 1979, she was re-engined with twin 375bhp Cummins diesels and again in 1999 with twin 715bhp Volvo diesel engines. Since 1977 she has also been fitted with GPS and satellite navigation equipment and is at present owned and operated by her builder, Mr Brian Chapman. The *Jubilee Queen* operates out of Padstow each summer between mid-May and mid-September. She makes daily cruises around the offshore islands (weather and sea conditions permitting) where sea mammals and puffins are sometimes encountered. Also, on a high spring evening tide, she often cruises up the River Camel to Wadebridge, her port of construction. She is probably one of the few amenities in Padstow that isn't owned by Rick Stein!
Richard de Kerbrech

First published 2008

ISBN (10) 0 7110 3272 6
ISBN (13) 978 0 7110 3272 9

All rights reserved. No part o
by any means, electronic or 1
information storage and retri
writing.

© Ian Allan Publishing 2008

Published by Ian Allan Publi
an imprint of Ian Allan Publ
Printed by Ian Allan Printing

Code: 0810/B1

EAST SUSSEX COUNTY LIBRARY		
03573845		
Askews	Nov-2008	
387.234	£14.99	
2202002		

EXPLANATORY NOTES

Preceding each caption or group of captions is a block of technical and date information relating to the named and featured vessel or vessels. The layout of this information is as follows:

The vessel's name (with month and year first entered service), former names with the (year) in which the name changes occurred, the vessel's owners at the time photographed; the vessel's vital statistics: gross tonnage; overall length and beam in feet and inches with the equivalent (metric values); the vessel's builders and shipyard location; the engine installation, the engine builders and, where known, the horsepower output.

Note that for paddle vessels there are two possible beam dimensions – the breadth across the vessel's buoyant hull and the maximum breadth across the ship's structure, including the paddle sponsons.

ABBREVIATIONS

Throughout, the following abbreviations have been adopted:

2SA	Two-stroke Single Acting
4SA	Four-stroke Single Acting
auw	all-up weight
bhp	brake horsepower
CP	controllable pitch
cyl	cylinders
DR	double reduction
fld	full-load displacement tonnage
ft	feet
grt	gross registered tonnage
ihp	indicated horsepower (a calculated horsepower, nominally reckoned as 87 per cent of brake horsepower)
in	inches
lbp	length between perpendiculars
loa	length overall
LP	low pressure
m	metres
nhp	nominal horsepower
rhp	registered horsepower (reckoned as 83 per cent of indicated horsepower)
RoRo	roll-on roll-off
shp	shaft horsepower
SR	single reduction
VP	variable pitch
RP	reverse pitch

Introduction

Ferries operate around the world wherever there is a need to reach inaccessible communities on offshore islands or across river estuaries, or to maintain links between international ports – they are the only remaining passenger-carrying vessels that work regular schedules. Thanks to its geography – a combination of numerous inhabited offshore islands, a long coastline and countless river estuaries, both large and small – the United Kingdom characteristically fits this description, having an extensive network of regular ferry services employing a wide spectrum of craft types and sizes.

There are large short-sea ferries, maintaining open-sea route links to continental Europe and Ireland, and numerous inter-island ferries providing all-year-round access to and between offshore communities. In the sheltered waters of the coasts and river estuaries, ferries provide the means to reach inaccessible locations, avoiding long, circuitous road routes, while closer to the major cities they operate rapid and frequent schedules for commuter traffic. In the summer months, many of these craft have traditionally offered pleasure trips or mini-cruises but there were also dedicated ferry-type excursion vessels working the coasts and rivers as well as some of the inland lakes. Some of these vessels ranked in size with the larger short-sea ferries of the day.

Ferries & Pleasure Steamers – A Colour Portfolio concentrates on the period from the 1950s to the early 1970s, a period of great transition in ferry shipping.

The traditional cross-Channel or short-sea packet boats of the past, the type that predominated up to the early 1960s, were characterised by elegant lines, high speed, steam-turbine propulsion and, in the highest class of accommodation at least, a quite luxurious standard of décor. In many respects, they resembled passenger liners in miniature. They were also well-found vessels. The English Channel, North Sea and Irish Sea are all renowned for the extreme sea states that can be experienced. Therefore, scantlings on these ferries had to be such that they could withstand the worst sea conditions that might be encountered.

Similar to those short-sea passenger ferries, but smaller in scale and more commonly propelled by steam reciprocating or diesel machinery, in some cases driving paddle wheels, were the all-passenger ferries that were engaged on estuarial or coastal routes throughout the same period.

From the late 1950s onwards, as private car ownership increased and the transition from rail freight to road haulage gathered pace,

there was a gradual migration to ferries that featured more and more sophisticated vehicle-handling capabilities. In parallel, vessel design tended to become increasingly functional at the expense of the more aesthetic qualities of hull form, while diesel power was almost universally adopted for economy of operation, coupled with the re-emergence of the Voith-Schneider propulsion system briefly flirted with on cross-Solent craft before World War 2. This new generation of multi-purpose vehicle ferries replaced the more graceful passenger ferries of the immediate post-war years.

To facilitate rapid loading and discharge of accompanied vehicles, ramps were installed as standard equipment at the bow and/or stern of new ships. Categorised as roll-on roll-off craft, the later vessels of this type, certainly those operating on inshore waters or across river estuaries, were true roll-through ferries, loading at one end and discharging at the other in order to achieve the fastest turn-round times.

The trend to vehicle ferries in turn prompted a demand for a new type of passenger-only ferry which could operate independently of the slower schedules enforced by vehicle-handling practices. In many parts of the country, thousands of daily commuters made their way to and from work in nearby coastal cities or needed to travel to city centres from outlying districts along the shores of major river systems. The emerging demand for fast shuttle services on these routes gave rise to the development and introduction of novel marine craft: amphibious hovercraft, hydrofoils and surface-effect or sidewall marine vehicles.

Driven by economies of scale, in keeping with the trend with other categories of merchant ship, ferries of all types have grown in size. This has continued right up to the present and some of the large modern ferries now on the continental routes are of a size that rivals that of the great ocean liners of yesteryear.

The one exception to this is, perhaps, those tiny ferries that work across the relatively short distances of sheltered waters or river crossings. For these services, size and capacity are of less importance than frequency of departures, which are invariably unscheduled. Typically, these craft are little more than single- or double-ended pontoons, self-propelled by using either their own screws or pulling themselves along tethered chains or cables, the latter known as link ferries or floating bridges.

Historically, the routes on which ferries were operated during the period under review here have been supported by forms of waterborne transport of one sort or another going way back in the very mists of time. But change, while not always for the best, as hindsight often reveals, has been inevitable and ferry services have not escaped the unstoppable roller-coaster of progress. The opening of the Channel Tunnel along with the deregulation of short-haul airline operations, leading to cut-price air fares, has had some impact on the passenger vessels working certain short-sea routes. Likewise, the construction of road bridges over river estuaries and to some of the more accessible offshore islands has hit some of the smaller ferry traffic, while the changing leisure and vacation expectations of the population have undermined, indeed largely eradicated, the once popular fashion for coastal pleasure excursions during the summer months. The main change, though, has been to combined vehicle/passenger transport away from passenger-only services.

One of the outcomes of these developments, as well as of the move from public to private ownership during the 1980s, has been the disappearance of many once familiar operating companies and the emergence of new concerns and consortia that have replaced them. Today, we live in the age of corporate imagery and branding, so that the proud liveries that ship-lovers were once equally well acquainted with have been replaced by gaudier colour schemes complete with self-proclaiming banners of ownership.

With its array of superb colour photographs, *Ferries and Pleasure Steamers – A Colour Portfolio* provides a pictorial review of the ferry and leisure craft scene of almost half a century ago. Depicting examples of most of the vessel types described here, it is a glimpse of the extensive network of British passenger shipping services that thrived in the immediate post-war period, continuing into the 1970s. Unashamedly, we offer another indulgence in pictorial nostalgia.

As before, we have drawn from the many superb colour photographs taken by Kenneth Wightman as well as the images of another photographer who was actively recording the shipping scene some 40 to 50 years ago, the late Philip Fricker. There are also contributions from the collection of slides gathered by Mick Lindsay. The majority of these pictures have never been published before. It should be noted that, while some of the views show certain ferries as they appeared in more recent times, all of these vessels were built prior to 1977 and most of the photographs were taken in the 1960s or earlier.

David L. Williams & Richard P. de Kerbrech
Isle of Wight, April 2008

Acknowledgements

John Bartlett, World Ship Central Record

Ian Boyle, Simplon Postcards

David Clark

Colin Elvers

Mariann Fricker, on behalf of the late Philip J. Fricker

Les Howard

Mick Lindsay

Jim McFaul

David Newcomb, London Borough of Greenwich

David Reed

Don Smith

The late Raymond Sprake

GKN Limited (British Hovercraft Corporation), East Cowes, Isle of Wight

Lloyd's Register Fairplay (Philip Simons & Leslie Spurling)

Southampton Central Library – Maritime & Special Collections

Bibliography & Sources

British Coastal Ships, D. Ridley Chesterton (Ian Allan Publishing, 1967)

British Railways Steamers and Other Vessels (Ian Allan Publishing, 1962)

British Railways Steamers of the Clyde, John Thomas (Ian Allan Publishing, 1948)

By Road Across The Sea – Atlantic SN Company, Miles Cowsil (Ferry Publications)

Clyde Steamers Remembered (Paddle Steamer Preservation Society, Scottish Branch, 1994)

Glory Days: Paddle Steamers, David L. Williams (Ian Allan Publishing, 2002)

High-Speed Marine Craft (Macdonald & Jane's)

International Register of Historic Ships, Norman J. Brouwer (Anthony Nelson, 1993)

Isle of Wight Ferries, John Hendy (Ferry Publications, 2002)

Merchant Fleets in Profile: British Railways Steamers, Duncan Haws (TCL Publications)

Merchant Ship Panorama, P. Ransome-Wallis (Ian Allan Publishing)

Passenger Ships of the Irish Sea, 1919–1969, Laurence Liddle (Colourpoint, 1998)

The Navvies – History of the General Steam Navigation Company, Norman L. Middlemiss (Shield Publications, 1999)

Red Funnel and Before, Ron B. Adams (Kingfisher Railway Productions, 1986)

Red Funnel – A Pictorial History, Michael Archbold (Red Funnel Group, 1997)

Royal Road to the Isles, Ian McCrorie (Caledonian MacBrayne, 2001)

Ship Recognition – Merchant Ships, Laurence Dunn (Adlard Coles Ltd)

Short Sea: Long War, John de S. Winser (World Ship Society, 1997)

Solent Passages & Their Steamers, Ken Davies (Isle of Wight County Press, 1982)

Warships of World War II, H. T. Lenton & J. J. Colledge (Ian Allan Publishing, 1964)

The World's Passenger Ships, Colin F. Worker (Ian Allan Publishing, 1967)

Lloyd's Register – various

Marine News – various

Mercantile Navy Lists – various

Talbot Booths Merchant Ships – various

www.clydesite.co.uk/clydebuilt

www.cyber-heritage.org.uk

www.miramarshipindex.org.nz

www.nationalhistoricships.org.uk

www.simplonpc.co.uk

Duchess of Hamilton

This view from the stern taken aboard the *Duchess of Hamilton* on 20 August 1968, gives a flavour of cruising the Firth of Clyde and along the Argyllshire lochs in the final days of the paddle and turbine steamers. Bracing but relaxing, and often well patronised, the trips also retained the charm of an earlier generation right to the end, characterised by elegant dining in the restaurant and fitting musical entertainment (accordions and fiddles) on the open decks. Note the day-trippers all wrapped up for their excursion, despite the time of year, and the complete absence of notices for passengers' guidance, safety and comfort. *David L. Williams*

Earl of Zetland
(8/1939) North of Scotland,
Orkney & Shetland
Shipping Company
250 passengers
548grt; 166ft 2in (50.70m) loa
x 29ft 1in (8.90m) beam
Hall, Russell & Company,
Aberdeen
Oil, 2SA 6-cyl, by British
Auxiliaries Ltd, Glasgow,
driving single screw:
840bhp

Launched just prior to World War 2, on 20 May 1939, the *Earl of Zetland* (Zetland is an alternative spelling of Shetland) entered service three months later on the Orkney and Shetland routes from Scottish east coast ports. She ran in consort with the 1937-built *St Magnus* but shortly after entering service she was taken up for war service on the Pentland Firth from Scrabster and within Scapa Flow. In the early 1950s, she was joined by the *St Ninian* and *St Ola*. Besides her passengers, she had a cargo capacity of 9,480cu ft for general cargo and livestock. She was not fitted with stabilisers so she must have endured some heavy crossings! In October 1971, she came under P&O Short Sea Shipping Ltd only to be sold in 1975 to J. Turner of Stanmore, Middlesex, and

renamed *Celtic Surveyor* a year later. She was resold to Cosag Marine Services, London, in 1980 and again in 1982 to Celtic Surveyor Ltd for adaptation into a restaurant initially located in London's Docklands. At present she is moored in the marina adjacent to the Northumbrian Quay, North Shields, as a floating nightclub-cum-restaurant under her original name *Earl of Zetland*. This photograph, taken in 1972, shows the *Earl of Zetland* alongside at Lerwick, working cargo. It defies belief that a ship so small helped to keep the passenger and cargo route open in all weathers to the most northerly islands of the British Isles, surviving the ravages of the Pentland Firth!
Phil Fricker

St Rognvald

(3/1955) North of Scotland, Orkney &
    Shetland Shipping Company
12 passengers
1,024grt; 244ft (74.36m) loa x 39ft 2in
    (11.94m) beam
Alexander Hall, Aberdeen
Oil, 2SA 7-cyl, Sulzer type, by William Denny,
    Dumbarton, driving single screw: 2,100bhp

Though she had accommodation for only
12 passengers, the engines-aft *St Rognvald*,
seen here at Aberdeen, had been intended
originally to have a capacity for 50. With the
St Ola and *St Ninian* already providing for the
bulk of the passenger traffic and the cargo
steamers *Amelia* and *Rora Head* about to be
withdrawn, the former for scrap, it was decided
to complete the new vessel as a dual purpose
livestock carrier-cum-ferry. In this form the
St Rognvald also took over the duties of the
1946-built *St Clement*, working a route from
Aberdeen to Kirkwall, Lerwick and return, a
round trip of four days' duration. Paid off for
disposal in 1978 as new ships came into
service, she became the *Winston* under the
ownership of Ramajim Shipping Company,
Panama. As such, she became a regular visitor
to Shoreham. Further changes of ownership
followed as she was renamed *Washington*
(1986), *Radia 10* (1990) and *Ras-Halague*
(1991). She was laid up at Las Palmas on
24 July 1993 where she remained idle for five
years, only to be broken up there, commencing
12 January 1998. *Phil Fricker*

Borodino

Borodino
(6/1950) Ellerman's Wilson Line Ltd
56 first-class passengers
3,206grt; 312ft (95.1m) loa x 49ft
(14.8m) beam
Ailsa Shipbuilding Company Ltd, Troon
Triple-expansion 3-cyl steam
reciprocating & LP turbine with
hydraulic coupling, by builder, DR
geared to single screw: 2,450ihp

When the *Borodino* was launched at Troon on
7 February 1950 as Yard No 468 she was the sole
vessel in a very large fleet designed to carry more
than 12 passengers. She was purpose-built with a
dedicated refrigerated capacity to carry cargoes of
dairy produce. So that she could claim any priority
given to the discharge of such perishable cargoes
she sported a grey hull rather than the company's
usual green, a simple expedient for recognising her
status. Her regular route was Hull–Copenhagen–

Århus–Hull, with fortnightly sailings from her
home port. She had a relatively short career of
only 17 years and it is possible that the stiff
competition offered by the Danish DFDS ferries
may have contributed to her early demise. She
arrived at Bruges, Belgium, on 18 July 1967 to be
scrapped. This photograph, taken in May 1963,
shows her working cargo alongside a quay at an
unidentified location. **Kenneth Wightman**

Tattershall Castle

(11/1934) British Railways Board
942 passengers plus motor vehicles
556grt; 209ft 7in (63.88m) loa x 33ft 1in (10.09m) beam, 57ft (17.37m)
  across the paddle sponsons
William Gray & Company, West Hartlepool
Triple-expansion 3-cyl diagonal steam reciprocating, by Central Marine
  Engine Works, Hartlepool, driving paddles: 1,200ihp

Up to six years prior to the opening of the Humber Bridge in July 1981, the passenger and vehicle ferry service across the River Humber between New Holland and Kingston-upon-Hull was maintained by the sister paddle ferries *Wingfield Castle* and *Tattershall Castle*, along with the later, similar but larger, though less powerful, *Lincoln Castle* which was built by A. & J. Inglis on the Clyde. The three vessels were commissioned by the London & North Eastern Railway, passing into British Railways ownership in 1948 after the nationalisation of the British railway network. Their design was quite distinct, conceived for a service where robustness and reliability were important considerations, with side access to a small open well-deck aft for vehicle stowage and a long passenger saloon forward of the bridge. Access to the enclosed passenger areas was through unusually large openings beneath the bridge. The 'setting-sun' scrollwork device and grille concealing the paddles was as much for decorative purposes as anything else because the paddle boxes were integral to the hull for the after run, partially enclosed by the side plating. Seen here while still in ferry service in May 1963, the *Tattershall Castle* was acquired for preservation as a museum ship in late 1975, by then laid up as a hulk. She is now berthed on the River Thames in the heart of the City of Westminster where she is a restaurant and pub, upstream of the *Queen Mary* and the *Hispaniola*. **Kenneth Wightman**

Duke of York

(6/1935) ex *Duke of York* (1942) ex *Duke of Wellington* (1946),
  British Railways Board
1,500 passengers (450 sleeping berths)
4,325grt; 357ft 3in (108.89m) loa x 52ft 3in (15.93m) beam
Harland & Wolff, Belfast
4 x steam turbines, by builder, SR geared to twin screws: 9,000shp

The *Duke of York* was launched on 7 March 1935 as a twin-funnel turbine steamer for the London, Midland & Scottish (LMS) Railway for the Heysham–Belfast service. She was fitted with a bow rudder and had a service speed of 21 knots. After serving as a troopship between September 1939 and June 1940, the *Duke of York* returned to commercial sailings. During 1942, she was commandeered for Admiralty service and renamed HMS *Duke of Wellington* as an infantry landing ship, reverting to a troopship in December 1944. Following this, in 1945, her original name was reinstated and she was refitted with a single funnel. In 1948, she passed from the LMS to the nationalised British Railways and was switched to the Harwich–Hook of Holland route. In May 1953, she was in collision in fog with the US cargo ship *Haiti Victory* in which her bow section was completely sheared off forward of the bridge. She was rebuilt with a more raked bow. Sold to the Chandris Lines of Greece in 1963 as the *York*, she was rebuilt during 1964 for cruising in the Greek Islands and the Adriatic out of Venice, as the *Fantasia*. She was scrapped at Piraeus in December 1975. This undated photograph shows the *Duke of York* moored alongside at the ferry terminal at the Hook of Holland. **Ray Sprake**

St Edmund

(12/1974) British Rail Sealink
1,400 passengers (671 sleeping berths) and 290 motor vehicles
8,987grt, 426ft 9in (130.07m) loa x 74ft 4in (22.65m) beam
Cammell Laird, Birkenhead
4 x oil, 4SA 8-cyl, by Stork-Werkspoor Diesel, Amsterdam, SR geared to twin screws; 20,400bhp

The RoRo ferry *St Edmund*, seen here in August 1977, and the earlier *St George*, were two of the most powerful British ferries for their size, reflecting a revolution in this type of vessel that was taking place on routes down the length of the east coast of England. They were commissioned for the Harwich–Hook of Holland daytime service but were provided with ample cabin accommodation to make overnight crossings when required and they worked in conjunction with the Dutch pair *Koningin Juliana* and *Prinses Beatrix*. Their greater size and improved loading capabilities enabled them to make 24-hour round voyages but the enhancements to operating efficiency were not reflected in the standard of décor or the style of on-board service, the former being

rather plastic and starkly modern while the latter was reduced to a single class following the arrival on station of the *St Nicholas* ex *Prinsessan Birgitta*. The Ministry of Defence acquired the *St Edmund* in 1983 and, renamed HMS *Keren*, she was used as a troop transport with the Falkland Islands Task Force the following year. Three years later, no longer required by the MoD, she was sold and converted back for ferry work, first as the *Scirocco*, then from 1989 as the *Rozel* of Channel Island Ferries. Since 2004, she has been sailing as the *Santa Catherine I* between Spain and Morocco. **Richard de Kerbrech**

Empire Parkeston

(5/1930) ex *Prince Henry* (1937) ex *North Star* (1940) ex HMCS *Prince Henry* (1946), Ministry of Transport
Passenger numbers not known
5,576grt, 385ft 6in (117.50m) loa x 57ft 2in (17.42m) beam
Cammell Laird, Birkenhead
6 x steam turbines, by builder, SR geared to twin screws; ship not known

The *Empire Parkeston* was originally built as the *Prince Henry* for the Canadian National Railways' eastern coastal service. One of a trio, all built by Cammell Laird, her sisters were the *Prince David* and the *Prince Robert*. In 1937, she was sold to the Clark Steamship Company of Quebec and renamed *North Star*. She was taken up for war service in December 1940 as an armed merchant cruiser (AMC) and renamed HMCS *Prince Henry* with the pennant number F.70. Considerable alterations were made to her, involving the removal of her superstructure accommodation while two of her foremost funnels were merged into a single uptake. Her after funnel was retained unaltered. Painted in battleship grey, she took on a more warship-like appearance. In 1943, her role changed to that of Infantry Landing Ship (medium) for the Sicily and D-Day landings. Because of her original passenger-carrying role she was transferred to the

Ministry of Transport in 1946 as a troopship. In this latter capacity she carried British Army of the Rhine (BAOR) troops on leave via North Sea ports, principally Harwich and the Hook of Holland, for the next 16 years. She arrived at La Spezia in Italy on 20 February 1962 for scrapping. This photograph, taken before 1958, unusually shows the *Empire Parkeston* alongside at Dock Head in Southampton. She is sporting her Ministry of Transport livery and beyond her is another troopship thought to be Royal Mail's *Asturias*. **Steam & Sail**

Essex Ferry

(1/1957) British Railways Board

12 passengers & 36–38 railway wagons

3,242grt; 399ft 11in (121.89m) loa x 61ft 4in (18.68m) beam

John Brown & Company, Clydebank

2 x oil, 2SA 6-cyl, Sulzer TS48, by builder, driving twin screws: 2,680bhp

The *Essex Ferry* was launched on 24 October 1956 as a sister train ferry to the *Norfolk Ferry*, both having some 1,132ft (345m) track to carry railway rolling stock.

Six months after she entered service the new terminal in Zeebrugge's outer harbour was opened to which she operated from June 1957. During 1972, along with the *Norfolk Ferry*, she was used to carry new rolling stock between Holyhead and Dublin for the Irish Republic's railways. After passing briefly to Sealink UK on 11 January 1979, she was laid up in the River Blackwater in 1982. In April 1983, she was scrapped, ironically, at Rainham in Essex. Her hull was not demolished but used as a salvage pontoon during the recovery of the *Alexander Keilland* oil rig which had capsized in the Ekofisk oil field in March 1980. Following this her hull was towed to Norway in June 1983 and scrapped.

The austere, somewhat utility lines of the *Essex Ferry* are those of a vessel with no frills or luxuries, designed purely for the carriage of railway rolling stock. She is seen here berthed at Parkeston Quay, Harwich, in June 1964 with goods wagons and a quantity of crates on her stern deck. Ahead of her is either of the Zetland Steamship Company passenger motor vessels *Koningin Emma* or *Prinses Beatrix*. *Mick Lindsay*

Cambridge Ferry
(12/1963) British Rail Sealink
12 passengers, 38 railway wagons
& motor vehicles
3,294grt; 403ft (122.83m) loa x
61ft 4in (18.68m) beam
Hawthorn Leslie, Hebburn-on-
Tyne, Newcastle
2 x oil, 2SA 7-cyl, by Mirrlees
National Ltd, Stockport, driving
twin screws: 3,750bhp

When completed the *Cambridge Ferry* was the last of four train ferries built to maintain the Harwich–Zeebrugge night service transporting railway wagons. During 1977, she was modified at a cost of £91,000 after which she could carry 25 more vehicles on an extended top deck, while her stern was adapted to permit her to dock at Dunkirk. On 1 January 1979, she was taken over by Sealink UK. She operated the last Harwich–Zeebrugge train service on 31 January 1987, and then switched to the Dover–Dunkirk route. She collided off Dover on

1 May 1987 with the ferry *St Eloi*; her damaged bow was repaired at Smith's Dock in North Shields. From 1988, she was laid up for a period before acting as relief ship on the Fishguard–Rosslare run. She was sold in 1992 to Sincomar Ltd of Malta for the Italy–Albania route and renamed *Ita Uno*. In 1993, she was renamed *Sirio* and eventually arrived at Aliaga for demolition. The *Cambridge Ferry* is shown under way in this undated photograph, but the rolling stock may be clearly seen in the covered deck aft.

Mick Lindsay

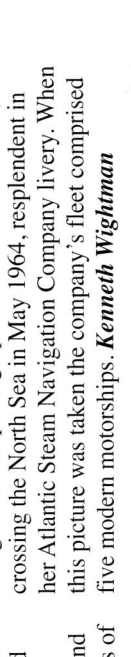

Doric Ferry
(2/1962) Atlantic Steam
  Navigation Company Ltd
35 first-class passengers and 100
  trailers
2,454grt; 361ft 6in (110.19m) loa
  x 55ft 1in (16.79m) beam
Ailsa Shipbuilding Company Ltd,
  Troon
2 x Vee oil, 4SA 16-cyl, by
  Davey, Paxman & Company,
  Colchester, driving twin
  screws: 4,000bhp

The *Doric Ferry* was launched on 27 October 1961 and made her maiden voyage on the Preston–Larne service in February 1962. She was later switched, along with the *Cerdic Ferry*, to the Tilbury–Antwerp and Rotterdam route. She was quite innovative with her RoRo facilities, fin stabilisers, bow rudder and twin rudders for confined waters manoeuvrability, reflecting the contemporary evolution of a type of vessel pioneered by her owners in the post-war period. On 18 November 1971, the company was sold to the European Ferries Group (better known as Townsend Thoresen) for £5.5 million and by 1976, the *Doric Ferry* had been repainted in the orange hull and blue funnel livery of the new owners. After 20 years of service, Townsend Thoresen, whose fleet had expanded with modern vesels, released the *Doric Ferry* and her sister as surplus to requirements. She was sold in 1981 to Compañía Armadora de Sudamerica and renamed *Atlas II* for service between Patras, Igoumenitsa and Brindisi. Later, she became the *Kapetan Alexandros* during 1989 under the management of Cycladic Lines and, again, in 1993 she was renamed *Kapetan Alexandros A*. It is thought that the photograph shows the *Doric Ferry* crossing the North Sea in May 1964, resplendent in her Atlantic Steam Navigation Company livery. When this picture was taken the company's fleet comprised five modern motorships. **Kenneth Wightman**

Edith

(1911) British Transport
Commission
Passenger numbers not known
283grt; 131ft 7in (40.11m) loa
x 28ft 6in (8.69m) beam
A. W. Robertson & Company,
Canning Town
2 x compound 2-cyl steam
reciprocating engines, by
builder, driving twin
screws; 48rhp

This Edwardian ferry was built locally for the London,
Tilbury & Southend Railway (LTSR) and had an open
foredeck for the carriage of horse-drawn vehicles and
cattle as well as for the few cars that were around in that
era. Her name was surrounded originally on both sides
of the bow with gold painted scrollwork and she had an
open bridge. She ran in consort with two smaller steam-
driven ferries, the *Catherine* and *Rose*. The LTSR was
absorbed into the Midland Railway in 1912 which itself
became part of the London, Midland and Scottish
Railway in 1923. In 1948, she was nationalised under
British Railways. Originally, she operated between
Gravesend and Tilbury Riverside but by 1957, to cater

for the ever-increasing passenger traffic, the Tilbury
Landing Stage terminal was opened. In 1961, when a
trio of new diesel-powered ferries came into service,
the *Edith* was retired, making her last crossing on
28 February 1961. She was renamed *Edith II* and,
together with the *Rose*, was towed to Belgium and
scrapped. Up until that time she had survived two world
wars and given 50 years of service on the River Thames
crossing. This photograph, taken in 1956, shows the
Edith bound for Tilbury with the World's End pub in the
background. Note that she still has an open bridge and
that her gold scrollwork has been over-painted black to
blend in with the hull. **Kenneth Wightman**

Edith

(3/1961) British Rail
Sealink/Sealink UK Ltd
340 passengers
214grt; 110ft (33.53m) loa
x 27ft (8.23m) beam
White's Shipyard
(Southampton) Ltd
Oil, 2SA 6-cyl, by Lister
Blackstone Marine,
Dursley, driving a single
Voith-Schneider
propulsion unit: 300bhp

This little diesel passenger ferry entered service on the busy Tilbury–Gravesend passenger service during March 1961 to join her sisters *Catherine* and *Rose*. The trio had a speed of 9 knots, adequate for the short Thames crossing. The *Edith* was built with six hydraulically-operated side gangways. She was propelled by a single Voith-Schneider propulsion unit for greater manoeuvrability in the tidal waters of the River Thames. Back in the 1960s, when Tilbury Docks was a thriving commercial area, many commuters with their bikes used this service; equally passengers would commute from Essex to south London and Kent via this route. Late in 1977, she was briefly seconded to Hull to replace the *Farringford* during her overhaul. In 1979, ownership of this service transferred to Sealink UK Ltd. With newer ferries coming on stream, the *Catherine* was laid up in 1981 as a standby ferry.

The *Rose* had already been sold, some 14 years earlier, to become the *Keppel* for Clyde duties. When, in 1984, the *Catherine* was withdrawn for eventual further service on the River Tyne as the *Latis*, the *Edith* carried on alone. In May 1990, Sealink UK passed to Stena and the *Edith* was chartered to them. Ownership changed again in 1991 when she passed to White Horse Ferries. With the delivery of the new ferry *Great Expectations* in 1992, the *Edith* was withdrawn and, as of June 2004, she was undergoing conversion to a private craft-cum-yacht at Greenwich. This photograph, taken in August 1977, shows the *Edith* having just departed Tilbury Landing Stage bound for Gravesend. Although it is the height of the summer season, she is clearly far from full.
Richard de Kerbrech

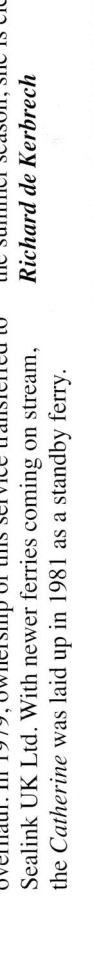

Squires

Squires

(12/1922) London County Council

Passenger and vehicle numbers not known

625grt; 172ft (52.42m) loa x 44ft (13.40m) beam, 62ft (18.90m) across the paddle sponsons

J. Samuel White, Cowes, Isle of Wight

Diagonal steam reciprocating, by builder, driving paddles: ihp not known

Prior to the introduction of the *Ernest Bevin* (below) and her two sisters in the early 1960s, the Woolwich Free Ferry service was maintained by the four paddle-driven vessels of the 'Squires'-class, all completed by the J. Samuel White shipyard between 1922 and 1930, the *Squires* costing £69,290. The Cowes shipbuilder was better known for naval vessels, but it also built the *Crested Eagle* for the General Steam Navigation Company, plus at least three chain ferries besides a number of coastal and short-sea ships for British Railways, including the *Caesarea* and *Sarnia* shown elsewhere in this book. Ferries like the *Squires*, *Gordon*, *Will Crooks* and *John Benn*, all coke-fired and manually

stoked to reduce smoke, were typical workhorses on various river crossings, providing years of uninterrupted and generally unnoticed local service. For the *Squires*, named after the one-time mayor of Woolwich, this amounted to almost 40 years through both peace and war until she was broken up at Bruges from 11 October 1963. She is seen here heading towards the terminus on the south bank of the Thames with the Woolwich power station in the background. The distinctive appearance of these craft with their tall, thin funnels can be clearly seen. Note, too, the raised car decks and the covered passenger access ways running along each side of the main deck.
World Ship Society

Ernest Bevin

Ernest Bevin

(7/1963) HM Government

1,030 passengers plus motor vehicles

738grt; 185ft 7in (56.56m) loa x 62ft 7in (19.08m) beam

Caledon Shipbuilding & Engineering Company, Dundee

2 x oil, 4SA 7-cyl with flexible couplings, by Mirrlees National Ltd, Ashton-under-Lyne, driving two directional propellers, 1 forward and 1 aft: 1,000bhp

By the early 1960s, the four White-built paddle ferries of the 'Squires'-class were reaching the end of their working lives, and were pretty much worn out after years of arduous service. The London County Council, as it still was at that time, ordered three replacement craft from the Caledon shipyard, delivered in 1963 as the *John Burns*, *Ernest Bevin* and *James Newman*. As with the earlier quartet, each honoured a prominent local politician. The *Ernest Bevin*, shown here moored in the river on 17 August 1996 though still running the Woolwich free ferry service, commemorated the Labour MP for Central Wandsworth and wartime Minister for Labour and National Service. The *Ernest Bevin* and her sisters are RoRo type ferries, having the car deck placed above the passenger deck to correspond with the linkspans at each terminus.

These craft are among the biggest vessels of this type operated on major rivers in the UK but have similar river ferry duties to, for example, the *Shieldsman* and *Pride of the Tyne* between North and South Shields and the *Yoker Swan* and *Renfrew Rose* across the River Clyde. Although the vessels are owned by HM Government, the service is operated by the London Borough of Greenwich.
World Ship Society

Queen of the South
(5/1931) ex *Jeanie Deans*
(1968), Coastal Steam
Packet Company
893 passengers
839grt; 257ft 10in (78.58m)
loa x 30ft (9.14m) beam,
59ft (17.98m) across paddle
sponsons
Fairfield, Govan, Glasgow
Triple-expansion 3-cyl
diagonal steam
reciprocating, by builder,
driving paddles; 2,200ihp

The former London & North Eastern Railway (LNER) paddler *Jeanie Deans* was possibly the most popular of the Clyde steamers. Her 33-year career in Scotland, interrupted only for war service as an auxiliary minesweeper and anti-aircraft vessel, drew to a close on 28 September 1964 with her final pleasure trip from Glasgow. Laid up that winter, she was offered for sale the following March and purchased by a consortium led by Erith businessman Don Rose. Renovated at considerable cost and fittingly painted in LNER colours, she was to operate summer cruises from Tower Pier to Southend, Clacton, Herne Bay and Whitstable in the Thames tradition, under the name *Queen of the South*. It was not to be, however. Beset by persistent

mechanical breakdowns and paddle damage, the 1966 season, launched with high hopes that 26 May, ended prematurely. In a bid to overcome the problems, her boiler was re-tubed but she fared little better the following year, suffering further machinery malfunctions. Having lost the patronage of disgruntled passengers and with debts mounting, she was reluctantly sold for scrap at Antwerp in December 1967. With her exteriors looking quite resplendent, the *Queen of the South* is seen moored in the Pool of London in August 1966, in a position on the north side of the river virtually parallel to that now occupied by HMS *Belfast* alongside the south bank. Cargo ships busily discharge at Hay's Wharf in the background. **Kenneth Wightman**

Royal Daffodil
(5/1939) General Steam Navigation Company
2,385 passengers
2,061grt; 313ft (95.40m) loa x 50ft 2in (15.29m) beam
William Denny & Bros, Dumbarton
2 x oil, 2SA 12-cyl Sulzer type, by builder, driving twin screws: 4,500bhp

The General Steam Navigation Company originated in 1824 running cross-Channel packet services from London and it was one of the earliest concerns involved in the Thames pleasure cruise business, establishing an enviable reputation with its 'Eagle' steamers. To complement its Eagle Line paddlers, modern screw-propelled diesel-engined craft were introduced with the first *Queen of the Channel* in 1935, operated from the following year under the New Medway Steamship Company banner after that concern had been taken over. She was joined by the single-funnelled *Royal Sovereign* from 1937 and the larger, twin-funnelled *Royal Daffodil* in 1939. The outbreak of World War 2 prevented the latter ship from getting into her stride but she excelled during the Dunkirk evacuation, carrying more men to safety – a total of 7,461 – than any other rescue vessel. Following the end of the war the *Royal Daffodil* was employed briefly ferrying BAOR troops between England and Germany, but she soon returned to the Thames excursion trade which was as popular as ever. Registered under the parent company's name and now sporting its house flag on her funnels, she survived into the 1960s until broken up at Ghent where she arrived on 1 February 1967. In this view of her dressed overall in the Thames Estuary her side blisters with attaching struts can be clearly seen. Note the vertical runners below the lifeboat davits, to ensure that, when lowered, the boats descended clear of the blisters.
Don Smith

19

Royal Sovereign
(7/1948) General Steam Navigation Company
1,910 passengers
1,851 grt; 288ft 4in (87.88m) loa x 53ft (16.15m) beam
William Denny & Bros, Dumbarton
2 x oil, 2SA 12-cyl Sulzer type, by builder, driving twin
screws; 4,500bhp

To all intents and purposes, the *Royal Sovereign* of 1948 was an exact replica of her namesake built by Denny in 1937 and sunk by a mine on 9 December 1940. The one distinction between them, perhaps, is that the post-war vessel carried a radar installation above her bridge. Operated as the Eagle Steamers, among the varied cruises offered aboard the *Royal Sovereign* and her consorts were trips to the wartime evacuation and invasion beaches in France. These were initially well patronised but declining passenger numbers in the early 1960s led to the withdrawal of the General Steam Navigation excursion steamers in December 1966 and the cessation of the company's involvement in this form of passenger shipping.

The *Royal Sovereign* was sold to Townsend Ferries which had her converted into the RoRo ferry *Autocarrier* for the Dover–Zeebrugge route. Drastically re-modelled and barely recognisable, with vehicle decks in place of her passenger saloons and a ramp fitted at the stern, her tonnage was reduced to 996 gross. Sold again in 1973, she was transferred to Italy where, with further alterations to her appearance arising from the restoration of passenger accommodation, she continued to operate as a passenger and car ferry under the name *Ischia*. Sailing between Pozzuoli, near Naples, and Casamicciola on the island of Ischia, her career continued until 2008 when, at 60 years of age, she was finally broken up.

Don Smith

Queen of the Channel
(5/1949) General Steam
Navigation Company
1,536 passengers
1,472grt; 272ft 1in
(82.93m) loa x 44ft
(13.42m) beam
William Denny & Bros.,
Dumbarton
2 x oil, 2SA 8-cyl Sulzer
type, by builder, driving
twin screws: 3,000bhp

The *Queen of the Channel* was built immediately after World War 2 to replace an earlier vessel of the same name lost during the evacuation of Dunkirk in 1940. Unlike her predecessor, which was similar in appearance to the *Royal Daffodil* (see page 19), the new vessel followed the style of the replacement *Royal Sovereign*, completed in July 1948. A distinctive characteristic of these General Steam Navigation excursion craft was the blisters which extended for 150 feet along each side of the hull, permitting expansion of the passenger accommodation and giving them greater stability in rough seas. After she had almost 20 years running pleasure cruises along the Thames and across the Channel to Boulogne, Dunkirk and Calais, the demand for this sort of excursion declined sharply and the *Queen of the Channel* was sold out of the GSN fleet in 1968, renamed *Oia*. Eight years later, in 1976, she moved on to become the *Leto*. She was finally broken up at Eleusis from 29 March 1984. The photograph shows her on 23 July 1955, while still in her prime, as she passes Gravesend's West Pier. In the background in the Tilbury Docks may be seen the Orient Line's *Orsova*, still with corn-coloured hull, and a P&O 'Strath'-class liner. **Kenneth Wightman**

Canterbury
(3/1929) British Transport
Commission
1,387 passengers
2,910grt; 341ft 6in
(104.08m) loa x 50ft 6in
(15.39m) beam
William Denny & Bros,
Dumbarton
4 x steam turbines, by
builder, SR geared to twin
screws: 930nhp

The *Canterbury* was specifically
designed for the Southern Railway's
'Golden Arrow' express service on
the route between Dover and Calais
and was launched on 13 December
1928. She was an improved version
of the *Isle of Thanet* which served
the same route. Her high turn of
speed of 21 knots ensured a regular,
reliable and rapid service to
maintain the prestigious London–
Paris rail link. Although the service
was suspended during World War 2,
the *Canterbury* made a crossing in
1944 to bring HRH The Princess Marina to England for
her marriage to the late Duke of Kent. In 1947, she was
succeeded on the 'Golden Arrow' service by the newer
4,191grt steamer *Invicta*. Her later career saw her
switched between the Dover–Calais and Folkestone–
Calais routes and she also provided regular summer
services between Folkestone and Boulogne. After 36

years' service she arrived at Willebroek on 1 August 1965
to be scrapped. The photograph shows the *Canterbury*
alongside the quay at Boulogne on 16 September 1957,
some 28 years after she entered service, when a first-class
single on the 'Golden Arrow' from London to Paris had
cost £5. She still has an air of class about her.
Kenneth Wightman

Maid of Kent
(5/1959) British Rail
Sealink
1,000 passengers
(8 sleeping berths) & 180
motor vehicles
4,413grt; 373ft 1in
(113.71m) loa x 60ft 3in
(18.37m) beam
William Denny & Bros,
Dumbarton
2 x steam turbines, by
builder, DR geared to twin
screws: 11,500shp

At the time of her entry into service, the stern-loading
Maid of Kent was British Railways' largest passenger/car
ferry. She revived the name of an earlier vessel sunk on
21 May 1940 during the evacuation of Dieppe.
Introducing a new generation of state-owned ferries on
the Dover–Boulogne run, the *Maid of Kent* had
comfortable, modern interiors. She had two continuous
decks, the lower main deck
providing the vehicle stowage area
along with a mezzanine. Above
this, the main passenger
accommodation was located on the
promenade deck, comprising a
restaurant, lounge-buffet with self-
service cafeteria, a bar and smoke
room and a separate ladies' room.
Other design features included a
bow thruster unit, twin rudders and
fin stabilisers. Late on in her short

career of just 23 years, the *Maid of Kent* spent periods as
relief boat on the Weymouth–Cherbourg, Stranraer–Larne
and Fishguard–Rosslare routes. She was broken up at San
Esteban de Pravia, northern Spain, where she arrived for
demolition on 21 April 1982. Here, in April 1976, she
steams out of Calais into the mist, bound for Folkestone.
Richard de Kerbrech

Free Enterprise II
(5/1965) Townsend
Thoresen
1,000 passengers., 200 cars
4,122grt; 354ft 9in
(108.10m) loa x 60ft 4in
(18.40m) beam
NV Werft Gusto,
Schiedam, Netherlands
2 x oil, 4SA 12-cyl Smit-
MAN, by J. & K. Smit
Mach, Kinderdijk,
driving twin screws:
7,700bhp

Townsend Brothers had posed a real threat to its rivals British Railways and SNCF right from when its first purpose-built car ferry *Free Enterprise* entered service on the Dover–Calais route in 1962. She was joined on this run in May 1965 by the *Free Enterprise II*. Later, in March 1966, the vessel opened the new Dover–Zeebrugge route which rapidly expanded between then and 1976. In 1968, Townsend Brothers Ferries merged with Thoresen to form the new force on the Channel route, Townsend Thoresen. Between 1970 and 1974 *Free Enterprise II*, operated on the Southampton–Cherbourg route along with her 'Viking'-class consorts during the summers. Her final sailing out of Dover was in

spring 1980 before she was chartered to Sealink UK for summer operation on the Portsmouth–Cherbourg run prior to being laid up. She was sold in 1982 to NAVARMA/Moby of Naples and renamed *Moby Blu* for use on the Italy–Bastia, Corsica, run. In 2000, she was operating on the Piombino–Portoferraio (Elba) route but was inactive the following year. In 2003, she became the *Moby B* only to be sold for scrap, arriving at Alang in India on 16 December 2003 for demolition.
The *Free Enterprise II* is seen under way at speed in the English Channel whilst on the Southampton–Cherbourg service. *Ray Sprake*

Swift
(4/1969) Hoverlloyd
250 passengers and 30 motor vehicles
173 tons auw: 130ft 2in (39.67m) loa x
76ft 10in (23.41m) beam, across inflated
skirts
British Hovercraft Corporation, East
Cowes, Isle of Wight
4 x Marine Proteus gas turbines, by Rolls-
Royce, Coventry, each connected via
horizontal and vertical transmission
systems to nacelles with 19ft diameter
VP/RP airscrews: 17,000shp

After successful initial experiments, a quite basic
trans-Solent service using the small amphibious
SR.N2 hovercraft was started from an Isle of
Wight beachhead. Isle of Wight-based aircraft
manufacturers Saunders-Roe, which had
pioneered this technology and later restyled itself
as British Hovercraft Corporation, also saw the
potential for all-year-round passenger and
passenger/vehicle hovercraft operations across
both sheltered waters, such as the Solent, and on
longer, open-sea routes like the English Channel.
For the latter, the large SR.N4 craft was
developed, initially delivered (two for British Rail

Seaspeed and three for Hoverlloyd) in the Mk 1
configuration. All five were later upgraded to
either Mk 2 or Mk 3 (Super-Four) standard. This
view shows the first Hoverlloyd craft *Swift* at full
speed of 70 knots at a mean hover height of some
5 feet (1.5m). Sister craft were the *Sure*,
Sir Christopher (named in honour of
Sir Christopher Cockerell, inventor of the
hovercraft), both of which, with the *Swift*, were
upgraded to Mk 2 standard, and *The Prince of
Wales*. These craft operated from Pegwell Bay,
Ramsgate, to Calais.
British Hovercraft Corporation

The Prince of Wales
(1977) Hoverlloyd
278 passengers and
34 motor vehicles
200 tons auw; 130ft 2in
(39.67m) loa x 78ft
(23.77m) beam, across
inflated skirts
British Hovercraft
Corporation, East
Cowes, Isle of Wight
4 x Marine Proteus gas
turbines, by Rolls-
Royce, Coventry, each
connected via horizontal
and vertical transmission
systems to nacelles with
19ft diameter VP/RP
airscrews: 17,000shp

In October 1981, British Rail Seaspeed and Hoverlloyd merged to form a single cross-Channel operator, Hoverspeed, with a total fleet of four SR.N4 Mk 2s and two SR.N4 Mk 3s. The latter craft measured 185 feet (56.38m) by 92 feet (28.04m) and had up-rated Type 15M/529 Rolls-Royce Marine Proteus gas turbines producing a maximum of 19,000 shaft horsepower. Their payload was 424 passengers and 55–60 cars. Hoverspeed continued to maintain regular services between Dover, Ramsgate, Boulogne and Calais until October 2000 when the final Channel crossing by hovercraft was made, ending a consistent, 30-year-long service with this alternative form of transport. In the event a number of factors had conspired against hovercraft services: crossings in rough weather could be particularly uncomfortable and the craft were expensive to maintain,

a matter exacerbated by their regulation as aircraft under Civil Aviation Authority (CAA) rules. British Hovercraft Corporation also failed to build replacement craft, even though the BH.88 design had been on the drawing-board. The company had elected to terminate its hovercraft production line due to difficulties sustaining a viable business on the 'feast and famine' sporadic orders it received for new craft. Going back 23 years to 1977, this view shows the interior of Hoverlloyd's *The Prince of Wales*, newly completed as a Mk 2 SR.N4, on the Columbine slipway at East Cowes while opened to the public prior to her delivery. She appears to have the number GH-2012 on her side, although her official designation was GH-2054. *The Prince of Wales* was gutted by fire on the Dover slipway on 2 March 1993.
David L. Williams

Twickenham Ferry
(7/1934) Société Anonyme de
Navigation Angleterre-Lorraine-
Alsace (ALA)

500 first- & second-class
passengers and 130 cars, or 10
passenger rail coaches, 40
wagons and 25 cars

2,839grt; 366ft (105.70m) loa x
60ft 8in (18.50m) beam

Swan Hunter & Wigham
Richardson, Newcastle upon
Tyne

2 x steam turbines, by builder, SR
geared to twin screws: 4,900shp

The *Twickenham Ferry* was built as one of a trio of
innovative train ferries which inaugurated the
Dover–Dunkirk train ferry service on 12 October
1936. She originally carried the through train with
12 international sleeping cars that ran between
London and Paris. Alternatively she could carry
24 x 40ft wagons. For this she was equipped with
four lines of rail tracks on the lower deck which
converged into two tracks by which trains were
rolled off to the shore across the stern ramp and
linkspan. In addition to these there was a garage for
25 cars on the upper deck. The *Twickenham Ferry*
was handed over to the French in 1937 while her
sisters remained with the Southern Railway. In 1940,
after escaping the German advance into Dunkirk,

she was commandeered for service as a military
train and vehicle ferry, working between Stranraer
and Larne, later Southampton and Cherbourg,
whereas her two sisters served as auxiliary
minelayers. She was originally a coal-burner with a
mechanical stoker but after the war, in 1947, she was
converted to burn oil by which time she had been
handed back to the French to resume the rail service.
After nearly 40 years in service the
Twickenham Ferry was withdrawn and arrived at
San Esteban de Pravia on 26 May 1974 for
demolition. This photograph shows the
Twickenham Ferry in her ALA colours (note the
insignia displayed on her funnel) prior to the
adoption of Sealink livery. *Mick Lindsay*

Whippingham

(5/1930) British Transport
   Commission
1,183 passengers
825grt; 254ft (77.41m) loa
   x 30ft 2in (9.20m) beam,
   59ft (17.98m) across
   paddle sponsons
Fairfield, Govan, Glasgow
Compound 2-cyl diagonal
   steam reciprocating, by
   builder, driving paddles:
   1,650ihp

Sister ship of the *Southsea*, lost during World
War 2, the *Whippingham* and her consort were the
largest paddle steamers to be ordered and
operated by the Southern Railway between
Portsmouth harbour and the Isle of Wight. The
pair were built to serve primarily as excursion
steamers, their greater size suiting this role, but
their early careers were marred by breakdowns,
groundings and paddle-wheel damage. Just prior
to the outbreak of World War 2 they made a series
of special evacuation passages, ferrying school-
children from Portsmouth and Gosport to the
relative safety of the Isle of Wight, supported in
these duties by the newer *Sandown* and *Ryde*.
War service for the *Whippingham*, as for her sister
Ryde, was as an
auxiliary minesweeper in 1941–2. Thereafter, she
served as an auxiliary anti-aircraft vessel until the war's
end. Under the ownership of British Railways, the
Whippingham continued to fill the combined
ferry-cum-excursion steamer role she had been conceived

for but, coal-fired throughout her life, her engines made
her expensive to operate and maintain and she was retired
at the end of the 1962 summer season. She was broken up
at Antwerp where she arrived for scrapping to commence
in August 1963. *CCQ*

Sandown

(6/1934) British Railways
   Board
974 passengers (summer
   loading – reduced in
   winter)
684grt; 223ft (67.96m) loa
   x 39ft (11.89m) beam,
   52ft (15.85m) across
   paddle sponsons
William Denny & Bros.,
   Dumbarton
Triple-expansion diagonal
   steam reciprocating, by
   builder, driving paddles:
   1,047ihp

The third of four large, modern paddle steamers
commissioned in the 1930s by the Southern Railway for
its Portsmouth Harbour and Southsea to Ryde Pier
service, the *Sandown* and the later but very similar *Ryde*
featured triple-expansion steam engines and had a
distinctive cruiser stern. Launched on the Clyde on 1 May
1934, the *Sandown* replaced the old *Duchess of Kent*
which was sold to the New Medway Steam Packet
Company to become the *Clacton Queen*. Apart from ferry
duties, the *Sandown* was engaged on occasional pleasure
trips one of which, on 28 April 1935, took passengers to
greet the giant new French
liner *Normandie* as she
made her maiden arrival in
The Solent. War service for
the *Sandown* involved
participation in the Dunkirk
evacuation followed by
naval service as leader of

the 10th Minesweeping Flotilla (pennant number J.20).
She was back on station working the cross-Solent ferry
routes by late 1945. Though coal-fired throughout her
career, the *Sandown* continued to work alongside the new
twin-screw motorships of the 'Southsea'-class until
withdrawn from service and broken up at Antwerp from
16 July 1966. This view shows her entering Portsmouth
harbour on 1 August 1963. The *Ryde* has survived her by
more than 40 years but is now no more than a decaying
hulk at Binfield on the River Medina, Isle of Wight.
World Ship Society

Brading

(11/1948) British Rail
Sealink
1,331 passengers
837grt; 200ft 3in (61.04m)
loa x 46ft 8in (14.22m)
beam
William Denny & Bros,
Dumbarton
2 x oil, 2SA 8-cyl, by
Sulzer Bros, Winterthur,
driving twin screws:
1,900bhp

The *Brading* was launched on 11 March 1948 and joined her sister the *Southsea* on the Portsmouth–Ryde route in December of that year. With her sister, she was the first screw-propelled vessel on the route since the 1870s and only the second diesel-driven ferry. Her squat funnel and tripod mast were in contrast to the style of the traditional paddle steamers that still plied that route. The *Brading* and her sister were among the first cross-Solent ferries to be fitted with radar which, together with her enhanced sea-keeping qualities, made her an all-weather ship, vital for the maintenance of the all-year-round schedule between the Isle of Wight's railway network and the Portsmouth–Waterloo service. In 1967, she was fitted

with a stovepipe extension to her funnel and the following year the funnel casing height was raised to enclose this feature. At the beginning of the 1990s, with the introduction of the 'fast cats' *Our Lady Pamela* and *Our Lady Patricia*, the era of the post-war ferries was eclipsed. After many changes of livery and company branding, the *Brading* was scrapped during 1994 at John Pound's yard at Portsmouth after 46 years of sterling service. This photograph shows the *Brading* in August 1969 arriving at Ryde Pier on the Isle of Wight, packed with holidaymakers, day-trippers and commuters.

Ray Sprake

Shanklin
(5/1951) British Railways Sealink
1,377 passengers (summer
loading – reduced in winter)
986grt; 200ft 4in (61.05m) loa x
47ft 8in (14.52m) beam
William Denny & Bros,
Dumbarton
2 x oil, 2SA 8-cyl, by Sulzer
Bros, Winterthur, driving twin
screws: 1,900bhp

Whereas rivals Red Funnel had introduced screw-propelled motorships on its cross-Solent route prior to World War 2, British Railways did not introduce equivalent vessels on the Portsmouth–Ryde passage until late in the 1940s. These took the form of the three-ship 'Southsea'-class. Sturdy vessels of a broad-beamed design, they were excellent sea boats and went on to give their owners over 30 years of reliable service. When they first entered service, they were two-class vessels featuring art deco styling with Lloyd Loom seats and tables.

The *Shanklin*, the last of the three, arrived on station three years later than the earlier pair, *Brading* and *Southsea*, taking the name of a former BR paddler that had moved to Cozens & Company as the *Monarch*. The *Shanklin* was sold in 1981 for adaptation for pleasure cruises under the name *Prince Ivanhoe*. The venture did not last long, though, for she was wrecked during her first season, on 3 August 1981, while cruising off the Gower Peninsula, South Wales. Here the *Shanklin* is seen entering Portsmouth Harbour in November 1974. **Ray Sprake**

Caedmon

(7/1973) Sealink UK Ltd
756 passengers and 76 cars
764grt; 197ft 10in (57.92m)
loa x 51ft 6in (15.68m)
beam
Robb Caledon, Dundee
2 x oil, 4SA 6-cyl, by Mirrlees
Blackstone, Stamford,
driving twin Voith-
Schneider propulsion units:
1,980bhp

By the late 1960s, the demand for vehicle as well as passenger ferries on the Isle of Wight's Lymington–Yarmouth and Portsmouth–Fishbourne routes had increased enormously. In order to handle the growing volume of traffic Sealink ordered three sister ferries, the *Cenred, Cenwulf* and *Caedmon*, all named after celebrated characters from Anglo-Saxon times. When the *Caedmon* entered service in 1973, she was placed on the Portsmouth–Fishbourne route along with the earlier ferries *Camber Queen* and *Fishbourne*. In 1977, she went to Poplar to be fitted with an extra mezzanine deck to take 24 extra cars. When Sealink's new

St Catherine came into service in July 1983, the *Caedmon* was switched to the Lymington–Yarmouth route where she joined her two sisters. However, with the imminent introduction of the much larger Croatian-built ferries on that route, some if not all the vessels of the 'C' class are to be withdrawn from service (during 2009). This photograph shows the *Caedmon* in May 1981 discharging vehicular traffic at the Fishbourne terminal prior to its later reconstruction. Note her grey/blue funnel colours compared with the red/black colour scheme of the *Lymington* (page 50).

Ray Sprake

Cuthred
(6/1969) British Rail Sealink
400 passengers and 48 cars
704grt; 196ft 1in (59.77m) loa
x 51ft 7in (15.72m) beam
Richards (Shipbuilders) Ltd,
Lowestoft
2 x oil, 4SA 8-cyl, by English
Electric Diesels (Paxman
Engineeering Division),
Colchester, driving twin
Voith-Schneider propulsion
units: 1,500bhp

In 1961, the then rather quiet Portsmouth–Fishbourne route was served by just two ferries capable of carrying 70 cars between them. The ensuing rapid increase in vehicular traffic prompted British Rail to order a third vessel, the *Cuthred*, which, with a 25 per cent increase in car-carrying capacity, entered service in 1969. She was built at a cost of £275,000. The name *Cuthred*, commemorating an Anglo-Saxon king of Wessex, marked a departure from naming ferries after local place names. On 1 January 1979, she passed to Sealink UK. Four years later, she became the standby vessel when the new *St Helen* entered service but was also used on the Lymington–Yarmouth route. By 1986, however, she was laid up at Lymington and on 23 March 1987 she

became the first RoRo ferry of her generation to be completely withdrawn from the service of Sealink British Ferries to which she had passed in 1984. Later, on 23 November 1989, she arrived on the River Tyne for proposed conversion into a stern-wheeler named *Clemtyne*. Instead, in January 1990, she was sold to Transportes Fluvias do Sardo (Transado) for service between Setúbal and Tróia in Portugal as the *Mira Praia*. This photograph, taken in June 1970, shows the *Cuthred* passing the garrison church on her way into Portsmouth harbour. Although throughout her career she underwent many modifications and changes of livery, this view shows her as originally built in the early Sealink colours. *Phil Fricker*

Ferry Queen
(1959) Solent Boating Company
Passenger numbers not known
69grt; 72ft (21.95m) loa x 19ft (5.79m) beam
Camper & Nicholsons, Gosport
Oil, 2SA, by L. Gardner & Sons, Manchester: bhp not known

The *Ferry Queen* along with her sisters *Vesta* and *Vita* was originally built for the Port of Portsmouth Steam Launch & Towing Company. In 1961, this company merged with the Gosport & Portsea Waterman's Steam Launch Company to form the Portsmouth Harbour Ferry Company and she passed into that concern's ownership. She maintained the harbour ferry service, mainly for commuting dockyard workers and their bikes, operating in consort with the newer *Portsmouth Queen* and *Gosport Queen* after they came into service in 1966. Surplus to requirements, she passed to the Solent Boating Company, following which she was sold to Thames Pleasure Craft Ltd in 1974. Around 1995, she passed to City Cruises, remaining with them until 2006 when she was laid up at Isleworth. In 2007, she was once more deployed on the River Thames and early in 2008 she underwent an overhaul for continued service. Her former consort, the *Vesta*, now operates the Tilbury ferry service. This view of the *Ferry Queen*, taken on 16 May 1969, shows her with a crowd of day-trippers on an excursion around the NATO fleet review of that year. Notice that there is very little protection for her passengers apart from the awning because Gosport ferries were originally open-deckers, a design that had not changed radically for 80 years. **Phil Fricker**

Southsea Queen
(1974) Portsmouth Harbour Ferry Company
250 passengers
119grt; 75ft 2in (22.91m) loa x 25ft 1in (7.65m) beam
James & Stone, Brightlingsea
Oil, 2SA 6-cyl, by L. Gardner & Sons, Manchester, driving two Schottel propulsion units: 150bhp

The *Southsea Queen* was built as an addition to the Portsmouth Harbour Ferry fleet which then comprised the *Portsmouth Queen* and *Gosport Queen*, both of which had entered service in 1966, and the larger *Gay Enterprise* – later renamed *Solent Enterprise* – introduced in 1971. The foursome maintained regular services across Portsmouth harbour between the Hard and Gosport landing stage and summer excursion work in the environs of The Solent and Spithead. However, the *Southsea Queen* was disposed of after just four years, because it was said she was too small for these latter duties. Sold to the Hythe Ferry Company (White Horse Ferries) in 1978 she performed similar ferry work carrying commuters, shoppers and tourists between Hythe Pier and Southampton's Town Quay. Renamed *Hythe Hotspur*, she also continued to undertake pleasure trips, usually in connection with the maiden visits to the port of new ocean cruise ships, as well as to Cowes on the Isle of Wight for the regatta week's firework display.

The *Hythe Hotspur* was withdrawn from service in 1995. A distinctive craft with a pronounced spoon bow, she is seen here as the *Southsea Queen*, arriving at Cowes on a day trip. **Richard de Kerbrech**

Isle of Sark
(1/1932) British Transport
  Commission
1,400 passengers
2,233grt; 306ft (90.40m)
  loa x 45ft (13.72m)
  beam
William Denny & Bros,
  Dumbarton
4 x steam turbines, by
  builder, SR geared to
  twin screws: shp not
  known

The *Isle of Sark* was one of a trio of steamers built for the Southern Railway in 1932 for its service from Southampton to the Channel Islands. She operated in consort with her sisters the *Isle of Guernsey* and *Isle of Jersey* and the company's cargo vessels such as the *Fratton*. The *Isle of Sark* could be distinguished from her sisters by her Maierform bow. She was also characterised by her low hull and square bridge. The three 'Isle'-class ferries plied one of the longest and at times the roughest and most hazardous of Channel passages in an era before radar and satellite navigation. During March 1934, while drydocked in Southampton, the *Isle of Sark* became the first ship to be fitted with experimental Denny-Brown stabilisers. With the German occupation of the Channel Islands in World War 2 the service was suspended and in

February 1941 the *Isle of Sark* was switched to the Fishguard–Rosslare route. Later that year she became a radar training ship based at Bideford. The cross-Channel service was resumed in 1946 and two years later she passed to British Railways ownership following the nationalisation of the railways. The *Isle of Sark* sailed for Ghent where she arrived on 7 April 1961 for breaking up. A month later British Railways terminated its Southampton–Channel Islands service, transferring to Weymouth. The distinctive two-funnelled profile of the *Isle of Sark* is shown photographed at Southampton in May 1959. She and her sisters maintained a regular and reliable service to the Channel Islands for 24 years.
Kenneth Wightman

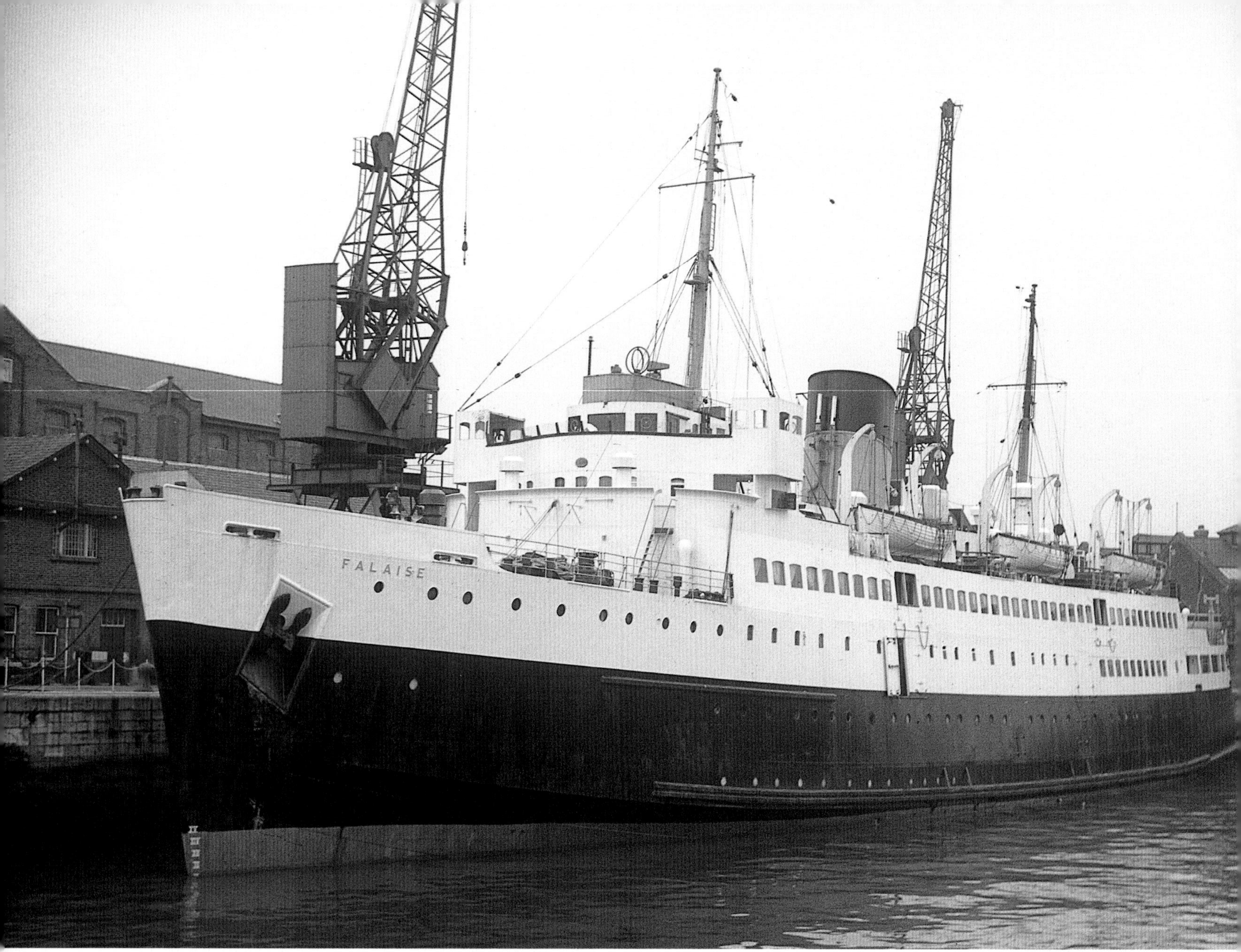
FALAISE

Falaise

(6/1947) British Transport Commission

1,400 passengers, 20 cars

2,416grt; 311ft 6in (94.94m) loa x 49ft 9in (15.16m) beam

William Denny & Bros, Dumbarton

4 x steam turbines, by builder, SR geared to twin screws: 8,500shp

The *Falaise*, named after William the Conqueror's birthplace, was launched on 25 October 1946. Ordered by the Southern Railway, she was placed in service on the Southampton–St Malo and Channel Islands run, making her maiden voyage on 14 July 1947. By 1960, she was working the Southampton–Le Havre route with the *Normannia* but, following the closure of British Railways' Southampton operations in 1963, she was switched to the Newhaven–Dieppe crossing. In 1964, she went to the River Tyne for a £350,000 conversion into a stern-loading car ferry with a capacity for 110 cars and 700 passengers, to operate the same route. While working this service she later had her funnel markings modified with the Newhaven Joint Service logo as the route was shared with French ferries. She went on to clock up some 300,000 miles on the Newhaven crossing. By the summer of 1973 she had been transferred to the Channel Islands car ferry run from Weymouth and her funnel was repainted with the Sealink logo. In 1974, she ran another all-year round service to the Channel Islands but by then was regularly plagued by engine trouble. Considered to be beyond economic repair, she arrived at Bilbao on 31 December 1974 for demolition. This striking picture, from the late 1950s, shows the *Falaise* in her original BR livery berthed alongside the Outer Dock at her home port of Southampton.
Kenneth Wightman

Right: Another view of the *Falaise*, this time showing her alongside the quay at Rouen with bunting flying. The photograph was taken on 27 May 1961 on a day excursion, probably from Southampton. Upon her entry into service she was the 43rd Southern Railway ship to come from a shipyard that had specialised in building for that company. Another influence on her name was that the Normandy town of Falaise had played a vital part in events following the D-Day invasion of Europe in 1944. The *Falaise* was thought by regular passengers of the day to be one of the most attractive of the cross-Channel vessels.
Phil Fricker

Earl Godwin
(6/1966) ex *Svea Drott* (1975),
Sealink British Ferries
982 passengers and 160 cars or 20
lorries & trailers
3,999grt; 325ft 5in (99.18m) loa x
60ft 2in (18.34m) beam
Öresundsvarvet A/B, Landskrona,
Sweden
2 x Vee oil 4SA 12-cyl. & 2 x oil 4SA
6-cyl. by Klockner-Humboldt-
Deutz, Cologne, SR geared to twin
screws: 12,000bhp

The *Earl Godwin* started life as the *Svea Drott* and
was launched on 20 January 1966 for Stockholms
Rederi A/B Svea, Helsingborg, to run between
Helsingborg, Copenhagen and Travemünde. She
was designed as a RoRo ferry with bow and stern
doors. In 1974, she was placed on the Stockholm–
Gotland route. In the same year, she was sold to
Lloyd's Leasing Ltd and chartered to Sealink UK.
Renamed *Earl Godwin* during 1975, she was placed
initially on the Portsmouth–Channel Islands route,
later switched to the Weymouth–Channel Islands
run. From 1984, she came under Sealink British

Ferries, as depicted here, following privatisation
of the former British Railways ferry services.
Her charter expired in 1990 and she was then sold
to Navigazione Arcipelago Maddalenino SpA
(NAVARMA) of Naples for use between Piombino
and Portoferraio (Elba), under the name *Moby Baby*.
This view shows the *Earl Godwin* at Southampton
in June 1988. Judging by her condition she may
have just completed a refit, her Sealink British
Ferries livery looking clean and smart.
Richard de Kerbrech collection

Dragon

(6/1967) P&O Normandy
Ferries – registered with
General Steam Navigation
Company

850 passengers (511 sleeping
berths) and 250 motor
vehicles

6,141grt; 441ft 8in (134.61m)
loa x 71ft 9in (21.87m)
beam

Dubigeon-Normandie SA,
Nantes – Chantenay

2 x Vee oil, 4SA 12-cyl, by
Pielstick, Nantes, driving
twin CP screws: 9,467bhp

At the time of her construction the *Dragon* was the first British passenger ship to be built in a French shipyard, at a cost of just over £2 million. Although completed by the above builders, she was originally laid down by Ateliers & Chantiers de Bretagne of Nantes at Prairie-au-Duc and launched there on 27 January 1967.

When she entered service between Southampton and Le Havre on 29 June 1967 she was the largest ship then operating on the cross-Channel ferry routes along with her French-flag sister *Leopard*. Together they operated a regular service for Normandy Ferries, an Anglo-French company part-owned by a subsidiary of the P&O Group. Fully air-conditioned and stabilised, they were well appointed with restaurant, cafeteria, two lounges and three bars. Subtle changes of ownership throughout her career meant she passed from the General Steam Navigation Company to P&O Normandy ferries, then to P&O Ferries. On 4 January 1985, she was sold to European Ferries. Refitted for her new owners, she was placed on the Larne–Cairnryan route under the name *Ionic Ferry*. Less than a year later, in January 1987, P&O acquired European Ferries and she once again came under the P&O banner. Later, in 1992, she was sold and renamed *Viscountess M*, later becoming *Charm M* (1995), *Memed Abashidze* (1997), *Med* (2000) and *Millenium Express II* (2000). On 2 March 2002, she caught fire in position 37° 21′ N, 21° 00′ E and subsequently arrived at Aliaga for breaking up. The *Dragon* is seen here in Southampton Water outward bound for Le Havre and painted in the post-1976 Normandy Ferries livery with its attractive light blue hull. *Phil Fricker*

Leopard
(4/1968) Normandy Ferries –
registered with Société
Anonyme de Gerance
et d'Armament (SAGA)
850 passengers (511 sleeping
berths) and 250 motor vehicles
6,014grt; 441ft 8in (134.61m) loa
x 71ft 9in (21.87m) beam
Dubigeon-Normandie SA,
Nantes – Chantenay
2 x Vee oil, 4SA 12-cyl, by
Pielstick, Nantes, driving twin
CP screws: 9,500bhp

The passenger/RoRo ferry *Leopard* was the second of
a pair of new vessels introduced by Normandy Ferries
on the Southampton–Le Havre route, the other being
the *Dragon* (see previous page). Construction of the
Leopard, like the *Dragon*, commenced at the Ateliers
& Chantiers de Bretagne shipyard where she was
launched on 3 November 1967. Completed by
Dubigeon, she was registered in France, while the
Dragon was registered under the British flag with the
P&O subsidiary General Steam Navigation Company.
The pair also worked their operator's Rosslare–Le
Havre route. Ultimately, the vessels came under the
full ownership of P&O Normandy Ferries, later P&O
Ferries, until the Southampton–Le Havre operation

was terminated in 1985. For the time, they were
excellent, well-appointed ships with a high standard of
accommodation. Access to the garage decks was via a
stern door and ramp. The *Leopard* is seen at
Southampton's cross-Channel ferry port in the former
Empress Dock in company with Swedish Lloyd's
Patricia (8,897grt; 463ft 3in/141.2m) which operated
on the Southampton–Bilbao route. After deployment
on other routes, the *Leopard* was sold in 1986 and
renamed *Countess M*. Fourteen years later, she became
the *Dimitra A*, then the *Mega 1* (2001) and *Talya 1*
(2002). She was broken up at Alang from 29 May
2004. ***Richard de Kerbrech***

Eagle

(5/1971) Southern Ferries
750 passengers, 200 cars
11,609grt; 466ft 3in
(142.11m) loa x 74ft 3in
(21.90m) beam
Dubigeon-Normandie SA,
Nantes – Chantenay
2 x Vee oil, 4SA 12-cyl
SEMT-Pielstick, by
Chantiers de
L'Atlantique, Saint-
Nazaire: 20,400bhp

Like the *Dragon*, the *Eagle* was ordered for P&O
subsidiary General Steam Navigation Company for
operation under the Southern Ferries banner. She was
launched on 16 October 1970 and entered service during
May 1971 on an innovative service between
Southampton, Lisbon and Tangier. A radical departure
from traditional ferries, she was in effect the first of many
'small liners' and inaugurated the direct ferry link
between the UK and North Africa. Despite her size she
still pitched and rolled during rough conditions in the
Bay of Biscay. She was often unfairly referred to as 'the
drug boat' because of her regular link with Tangier and
extra vigilance was exercised by Southampton's customs
each time she docked. In March 1975, she briefly came
under the direct management of P&O but on
19 December of that year the company sold her to
Nouvelle Compagnie de Paquebots of France which
renamed her *Azur*. In 1987, she was sold to Azur
Transportation Inc of Panama and renamed *The Azur*.
During the same year she was converted into a passenger
cruise ship. She became the *Eloise* in 2000 and the
Royal Iris in 2004. This photograph, taken in April 1975,
shows the *Eagle* loading at the quay at Lisbon. In the
background is the new Tagus suspension bridge which
had previously been named the Salazar Bridge.
Richard de Kerbrech

Princess Elizabeth

(8/1927) Red Funnel Steamers
700 passengers and 10 cars
388grt; 195ft (59.43m) loa x 24ft
(7.31m) beam, 48ft (14.63m)
across paddle sponsons
Day, Summers & Company,
Northam, Southampton
Diagonal compound steam
reciprocating, by builder,
driving paddles: 94ihp

This striking photograph shows the Red Funnel
paddle steamer *Princess Elizabeth* bound for
Southampton on 29 August 1958. To the left
background is the School of Navigation at Warsash.
Named in honour of the birth of the future Queen
Elizabeth II, when introduced in 1927 she was Red
Funnel's first fleet addition after World War 1.
She proved to be a versatile craft equally suited to
ferry schedules, summer excursions and tendering the
large ocean liners moored on the Motherbank. She
was capable of a top speed of 14.5 knots, achieved
during trials in Stoke's Bay. In fact, so successful was

she that, following the screw-driven motor vessel
Medina, Red Funnel ordered an almost identical
paddle ferry from Thornycroft at Woolston, delivered
in 1936 as the *Gracie Fields*. The later vessel, lost at
Dunkirk in 1940, benefited from the addition of a
bow rudder. The *Princess Elizabeth* was sold in 1967
for use as a marina clubhouse. Since then she has
been moved around in her retirement, spending a spell
on the River Seine at Paris and on the River Thames
at London. Latterly she has been berthed as a floating
restaurant and evacuation memorial at the French port
of Dunkirk. ***Phil Fricker***

Medina

(2/1931) Red Funnel Steamers

650 passengers

347grt; 143ft (43.58m) lbp x 30ft (9.14m) beam

John I. Thornycroft, Woolston, Southampton

2 x oil, 2SA 4-cyl, by Crossley Brothers, Manchester, driving twin screws: 890bhp

In the small diesel-powered *Medina*, Red Funnel aimed to bring into service a modern screw-driven equivalent of their leading paddle ferries of the time and in this respect she had comparable dimensions and overall capacity. However, she did not fulfil the company's expectations and subsequently the directors reverted to another paddle steamer in the next round of new construction. The *Medina's* flared bow was prone to berthing damage, making her unsuitable either for tendering work, then one of the mainstays of Red Funnel's business, or for high-season pleasure trips involving calls at many different piers. Likewise, her speed of just 11 knots made her the company's slowest ferry, a matter dealt with in 1953 when her original Gardner diesels were replaced with more powerful Crossleys. Nevertheless, she is remembered as Red Funnel's first screw-driven vessel, first diesel-powered vessel and first ferry to provide deck space for cars. She remained with Red Funnel for 31 years, replaced in 1962 by the passenger/car ferry *Osborne Castle*, when she was sold to Bland of Gibraltar to become the *Mons Abyla*. The *Medina* is shown leaving Cowes on the regular Southampton run in September 1958. As built, her funnel was white with a black top. The car stowage aft can be clearly seen, as can some passengers right up in her forepeak. *Phil Fricker*

Right: In 1971, the former *Medina* returned to the UK, spending a year in the Albert Dock, London, under the name *Marilu*. She then had a brief spell as a yacht club headquarters at Lymington Marina under her original name, as depicted in this view from June 1974. Three years later, having been renamed *Island Pride* in the interim, she was moved to Brighton Marina. Further moves took her to Newhaven and Rotherhithe. The *Medina* survived until September 1997, when she was broken up at South Shields when 66 years old – not bad for an 'unsuccessful' design. *Phil Fricker*

Vecta
(3/1939) Red Funnel
Steamers

855 passengers and 15 cars
630grt; 191ft 6in (58.36m)
loa x 30ft 2in (9.19m)
beam

John I. Thornycroft,
Southampton

2 x oil, 4SA 6-cyl, by
English Electric Diesels,
Rugby, driving twin
screws; 1,300bhp

Arriving at Southampton's Royal Pier in September 1965, with the warehouses on the Town Quay in the background, the *Vecta* completes another crossing on the Cowes–Southampton route in the final year of her Red Funnel career. Despite her age she still looks in good order. Launched in July 1938, her entry into service was delayed because of problems in obtaining the two Voith-Schneider propulsion units with which she was originally fitted. Intended to give her greater manoeuvrability, indeed to permit her to turn a full circle in her own length, they proved to be a nightmare for her engineers especially when her stock of spares, obtained from Germany, was destroyed in a wartime air-raid. She was dogged by breakdowns, which even prevented her participation in the Dunkirk troop evacuation, and the propulsion units were replaced with conventional screws and twin rudders for her return to full commercial service in February 1946.

Her enclosed car deck extended forward from beneath the bridge and can be seen through the large side ports. Sold to Townsend Car Ferries barely days after this photograph was taken, she was chartered to P. & A. Campbell for West Country pleasure cruising under the name *Westward Ho*. In preparation, her car deck was converted into a second saloon and her funnel fitted with a Campbell cowl. Painted in Campbell's distinctive black and white colours, she returned to service in 1966. Laid up in 1971 because of engine problems, she was sold a year later to Compass Catering and berthed at the Pomona Dock, Salford, Manchester, as the floating restaurant and nightclub *North Westward Ho*. In 1985, she was on the move again, subsequently turning up at different times at docks on the Wirral peninsular and the rivers Medway and Thames, in London's Docklands, until broken up in Cornwall in 1996.

Ray Sprake

Balmoral
(11/1949) Red Funnel
Steamers
892 passengers, 12 cars
688grt; 203ft 6in (62.03m)
loa x 32ft (9.75m) beam
John I. Thornycroft,
Southampton
2 x oil, 2SA 6-cyl, by
Newbury Diesel, driving
twin screws: 1,200bhp

When launched on 27 June 1949, the *Balmoral* was the second ship in the Red Funnel fleet to bear the name and the company's first ferry to be completed following World War 2. Red Funnel's third motor vessel, she had been designed as a service ship with excursion and tender capabilities. She had a semi-enclosed deck aft which could take up to 12 cars. One of the original facilities offered until 1959 was a dining saloon with waiter service. On 21 November 1961, the *Balmoral* collided with Sitmar Line's liner *Fairsky* in Cowes Roads. Her starboard lifeboat was crushed and she sustained a gash in her side from the deck to the waterline. At the time no

passengers were aboard. Later, during a thick fog in January 1964, she grounded off the Prince's Green, Cowes, and was towed off by the company's tug *Thorness*. When the fourth RoRo car vessel was introduced in December 1968, the *Balmoral* was withdrawn from use and in May 1969, she was taken up on long-term charter by P. & A. Campbell Ltd for service on the Bristol Channel. In this mid-1960s view, the *Balmoral* is embarking passengers for Southampton at Cowes Pontoon at the Fountain Pier. Cars were loaded on her afterdeck by wooden ramps. Note the complete absence of signs or notices. *Phil Fricker*

Carisbrooke Castle
(5/1959) Red Funnel Steamers
1,200 passengers, 45 cars
672grt; 191ft 2in (58.27m) loa x 42ft 2in (12.85m) beam
John I. Thornycroft, Southampton
2 x oil, 2SA 8-cyl, by Crossley Bros, Manchester; 1,800bhp

By the late 1950s, the demand to convey even more cars and commercial vehicles to the Isle of Wight, especially on the Southampton–Cowes route, had become critical. The converted tank landing craft *Norris Castle* was unable to cope with the growing traffic volumes. To meet the demand the *Carisbrooke Castle*, Red Funnel's first purpose-built passenger and vehicle RoRo ship, was launched by Lady Hobart on 27 November 1958. This radical vessel with its bow ramp and 13ft (3.96m) car turntable entered service on 23 May 1959. She was the first of a class of four similar vessels that would follow over the next nine years. Her initial itinerary was Southampton–Cowes–East Cowes, using the facility at Cowes Pontoon to land and load cars through her side doors over wooden ramps. Her pioneering days on the route were numbered when she was superseded by the much larger *Netley Castle* which entered service in June 1974. In September of that year she was sold to the Italian company Soc P Artenstea di Navigazione for service between Naples and the island of Ischia as the *Citta di Meta*. Sold again in 1989, she was renamed *Giglio Espresso II*. Between 2000 and 2004, she had two further Italian owners before being sold to Turkish shipbreakers, arriving at Aliaga in September 2007. The photograph

shows the *Carisbrooke Castle* approaching her Southampton terminal in October 1972, being overhauled by the hydrofoil *Shearwater 3*, Red Funnel's third hydrofoil, which had been in service for only five months. **Richard de Kerbrech**

Below: The *Carisbrooke Castle*, photographed on 6 June 1959, a fortnight after she entered service, showing her original appearance prior to being fitted with radar and having the boat deck extended to the stern with deckhouses over the stairways to the saloon deck. She is approaching Southampton's Royal Pier with her side doors on the car deck swung open. They were used for vehicle loading and discharge at West Cowes Pontoon and at the Royal Pier when the bow ramp could not be deployed. Note the builder's Thornycroft funnel cowl. In the background is Southampton's Ocean Terminal. **Phil Fricker**

Cowes Castle
(12/1965) Red Funnel
Steamers
900 passengers and 70 cars
912grt; 221ft (67.37m) loa
x 40ft (12.83m) beam
John I. Thornycroft,
Southampton
2 x oil, 2SA 8-cyl, by
Crossley Bros.,
Manchester: 1,800bhp

When originally built, the *Cowes Castle* measured 786grt and 191ft (58.21m) in length. She was the third purpose-built car ferry to enter Red Funnel service on the Southampton–Cowes–East Cowes route. She was designed to carry 500 passengers and 45 cars but after less than 10 years in service she was converted into a drive-through ferry between September and December 1975 at Boele's yard in Rotterdam, to increase her car capacity by 25. She was extended by 30ft (9.14m) and her car deck was raised 14ft (4.27m). Between them, the *Cowes Castle* and the similarly modified *Norris Castle* and *Netley Castle* managed to cope with the increased volume of traffic to the Isle of Wight until they were succeeded by the 'Raptor'-class ferries which entered service from October 1993, commencing with the *Red Falcon*. The call at West Cowes ceased altogether, leaving a direct car ferry service between East Cowes and Southampton. Following her last trip to Cowes on 18 March 1994, the *Cowes Castle* was sold to Jadrolinija of Croatia for service to islands in the Adriatic, renamed *Nehaj*. This view shows the *Cowes Castle* in her final Red Funnel livery, passing Netley en route for Southampton, a clear example of a ship whose function has over-ridden aesthetics! *Richard de Kerbrech collection*

Netley Castle
(6/1974) Red Funnel
Steamers

925 passengers and 80
motor vehicles

1,183grt; 245ft 6in
(74.82m) loa x 49ft 11in
(15.21m) beam

Ryton Marine, Wallsend-
on-Tyne

4 x Vee oil, 4SA 8-cyl, by
Caterpillar Tractor
Company, Peoria,
driving 4 directional
propellers, 2 forward and
2 aft: 2,260bhp

Ordered in January 1972, this RoRo passenger vessel
represented a major development in the vehicular ferries
operated on the Cowes–Southampton route, following the
earlier *Carisbrooke*, *Osborne*, *Cowes* and *Norris Castles*.
Unlike this quartet, three of which required modification,
she was provided with drive-through capability from her
inception. During the *Netley Castle*'s construction, Ryton
Marine went into liquidation but Red Funnel was
allowed, under sanction of the Official Receiver, to recruit
a team of shipyard workers in order to complete her itself.
It is interesting to note that she was the first Red Funnel
vessel since the *Medina* of 1931 not to be built by
Thornycroft. For some years after her entry into service,
until 1983, she was the largest ferry operating across the
Solent. The *Netley Castle* had two bridges placed above
and at either end of the passenger saloon. She was highly

manoeuvrable, each of her four propellers, operated in
pairs, being capable of rotation through 360 degrees.
She also had an athwartship-thrust propeller located in the
forward part of the hull. A self-steering system that was
installed during her build was later removed. As the last
Red Funnel ferry capable of loading and discharging at
West Cowes, her career was brought to an end in 1996
following the construction of new linkspans at East
Cowes and Southampton for the *Red Falcon* and the other
'Raptor'-class ferries. The *Netley Castle* left Southampton
on 24 January 1997 bound for a new career in the Adriatic
with Jadrolinija, Croatia, as the *Sis*. At Cowes on the
occasion of her entry into service, the *Netley Castle* is
seen with cream funnels with black tops. From 1980,
they were painted red with black tops. *Phil Fricker*

46

Shearwater 3
(5/1972) Red Funnel
Seaflight
67 passengers
61.9grt; 73ft 2in (22.30m) loa x 16ft 1in (4.90m) beam (across hull only)
Rodriguez Cantieri Navali SpA, Messina, Italy
MTU 12V 331 TC82 diesel, driving single 3-bladed propeller through Zahnradfabrik gearbox: 1,430bhp

Red Funnel first attempted to offer a fast, passenger-only service from Cowes to Southampton from 1933 using an RAF air-sea rescue-type launch named *Island Enterprise*. This did not continue beyond 1938 though, possibly because there was insufficient patronage. By the mid-1960s, it had become apparent that the volume of daily commuters and shoppers had reached a level that supported the reintroduction of such a rapid crossing service, besides which there was now local competition from British Rail's Seaspeed hovercraft. Launched in 1969 under the Seaflight banner, Red Funnel's high-speed service employed two small H57 hydrofoils supplied by Italian builders Seaflight SpA, but reliability problems forced the company to replace them swiftly with craft built by rival Messina concern Rodriguez. They were delivered from 1972, commencing with *Shearwater 3* seen here, and within ten years there were four sister RHS70 vessels on duty running regular schedules. With a cruising speed of 32.4 knots and a maximum speed of 36.5 knots, each of these craft carried 100,000 passengers annually over the 10.8-nautical mile/20-minute duration route. From the early 1990s, the Shearwater hydrofoils were progressively replaced by a new generation of high-speed craft, the four water-jet-propelled Red Jet catamarans. *Shearwater 3* was sold in March 1993 for further service in the Aegean Sea. *Richard de Kerbrech*

end of 1989 it had conveyed in excess of 10 million passengers. The amphibious capabilities of hovercraft are demonstrated here by an SR.N6 crossing ice. *British Hovercraft Corporation*

SR.N6 Mk 1
Hovertravel, British Rail Seaspeed and other operators
38 passengers
12 tons auw; 48ft 7in (14.80m) loa x 25ft 3in (7.70m) beam, across inflated skirts
British Hovercraft Corporation, East Cowes, Isle of Wight
Marine Gnome gas turbine, by Rolls-Royce, Coventry, driving 2.74m dia. Dowty Rotol 4-blade VP airscrew: 900shp

Operated by British Rail Seaspeed on the Cowes–Southampton route and by Hovertravel on the Ryde–Southsea route, as well as by other UK concerns, the single-engined SR.N6 was the most produced British hovercraft, some 42 in a number of variants having been built in the 1960s. They had an integrated lift and propulsion system, the single engine supplying power for both requirements. Though they were capable of a speed of 52 knots, they suffered from high levels of noise from both the engine and propeller, causing widespread environmental opposition. Whereas Seaspeed abandoned its Cowes–Southampton operation, Hovertravel replaced its SR.N6 craft from the early 1980s by the twin ducted-fan AP1-88 craft which also had greater capacity (80–100 seats) and more comfortable accommodation. Isle of Wight-based Hovertravel, an early pioneer of hovercraft ferry operations, carried around 600,000 passengers annually on its cross-Solent service and from its inception in 1965 to the

Nottingham Castle
(1943) ex *No.298*,
ex *Cresset* (1970),
Imperial Tobacco Group
Ltd
20 passengers
38grt/40fld: 60ft (18.29m)
loa x 14ft (4.27m) beam
Hancocks Shipbuilding
Company, Pembroke
Dock
Compound 2-cyl steam
reciprocating, by LNER
Cowlairs Works,
Glasgow: ihp not known

The minute pleasure steamer *Nottingham Castle*, moored in Cowes Harbour in September 1971, makes a contrast in size with the *Eagle* (on page 39), giving some idea of the broad spectrum of vessels that fall within the category of ferry or excursion ship. Built as *Steam Harbour Launch No.298* for the Admiralty, her initial duties may well have involved the conveyance of service passengers within the sheltered confines of one of the Royal Naval bases or dockyards. Unusually, her compound steam engines were supplied by the London & North Eastern Railway, no doubt a wartime expedient. It is not known when she was given the name *Cresset* but it may have coincided with when she was first sold to private commercial interests. The Imperial Tobacco Group acquired her in 1970 from Machin, Knight & Sons Ltd

of Southampton – the stylised JP on her funnel represents the John Player cigarette brand. She was engaged in private VIP excursion trips in connection with such events as the Whitbread Round the World yacht race, Cowes Week and other important maritime occasions, as well as trips further afield to the Bristol Channel, Pembroke and Cardigan Bay. Ownership of the *Nottingham Castle* by Imperial Tobacco was relatively short-lived for she was sold to Canadian interests soon after this photograph was taken. Her new owners, Upper Canada Steam Navigation Company, maintain her in operating condition as a private yacht at the Paignton House Hotel, Lake Rousseau, Ontario, offering her for charter for excursion trips.

Ray Sprake

Lymington
(5/1938) British Railways
  Board

516 passengers and 20
motor vehicles (summer
loading – reduced in
winter)

275grt; 148ft (45.10m) loa
x 36ft 9in (11.20m) beam
William Denny & Bros,
Dumbarton

Oil, 4SA 12-cyl, by
W. H. Allen, Bedford,
driving fore and aft Voith-
Schneider propellers:
400bhp

The *Lymington* was the first
double-ended car ferry to be
placed on the Yarmouth–
Lymington route, just prior
to World War 2. Drive-
through vessels had been
placed on the Portsmouth–
Fishbourne route some ten
years earlier in the form of
the diminutive *Fishbourne*,
Wootton and *Hilsea*.
The *Lymington* was
revolutionary for other
reasons, being the first
British ferry to have the
Voith-Schneider propulsion
system, enabling her to be
manoeuvred in all directions
without the need for
rudders. She is seen here in
the approaches to the
Yarmouth ferry terminal on
the Isle of Wight in August
1963. *Ray Sprake*

Lymington
British Rail Sealink

In this second view of the car ferry *Lymington*, she is seen loading cars at Yarmouth, Isle of Wight, prior to a return sailing to Lymington. The picture shows her painted in the freshly adopted colours of Sealink after the formation of that British Railways operating division in 1968 (in fact the Sealink name and logo were not adopted until 1970). In this view, looking across the open loading ramp, the restricted dimensions of her car deck space, limited to only 16 cars in winter, are evident. The scene is one of ferry operations in the days prior to the implementation of modern health and safety laws, evidenced by the absence of a safety barrier across the slipway, and the lack of quayside railings, dangers to which crew and shore staff alike appear completely oblivious. It is also an interesting snapshot of some British motor cars of the period. The *Lymington* survived until 1973, when she was replaced by the *Cenwulf*. New duties awaited her, however, and she was transferred to the Firth of Clyde for the Dunoon–Gourock vehicle ferry service of Western Ferries. Renamed *Sound of Sanda*, she celebrated the 50th anniversary of her completion in 1988. **Ray Sprake**

Farringford

(1/1948) British Rail
    Sealink
796 passengers and 41 cars
489grt; 178ft (54.26m) loa
x 49ft 10in (15.19m)
    beam
William Denny & Bros,
    Dumbarton
Diesel-electric, comprising
2 x oil 4SA 6-cyl,
connected to generators
and electric motors, by
English Electric, Stafford,
driving paddles: 660bhp
(550shp)

Although the *Farringford* had been ordered by the Southern Railway, the rail network had been nationalised by the time she was delivered and she entered service as a BR ship. Ideally, Voith-Schneider propulsion, such as that fitted to the pre-war *Lymington*, would have been best for the confines and constraints of the Lymington River but, because of difficulties in obtaining the German-made units, a paddle-vessel design was chosen instead. Thus, she had diesel generators driving independent motors on each paddle such that one could be reversed with the other driving ahead. Coupled with four rudders, this gave the *Farringford* great manoeuvrability and power. The Lymington–Yarmouth route was equally busy in summer and winter, patronised all year round by the island commuters travelling to the Wellworthy factory for the night shift. When the larger *Cenwulf* was placed on the Lymington–Yarmouth route the *Farringford* was transferred to Hull, on 15 January 1974, to replace the *Wingfield Castle* on the River Humber's Hull–New Holland service. She was modified so that cars could be side-loaded. She maintained this route until the Humber Bridge was opened in June 1981 when she was sold to Western Ferries on the Clyde. After only a brief diversion, she arrived back at Hull on 5 May 1984 to be broken up. Photographed on 26 July 1972, the *Farringford* approaches her Yarmouth terminal at speed. To the left is the excursion vessel *Bournemouth Queen* alongside Yarmouth Pier. As a paddler the *Farringford* was understated, but she was unique: a hybrid design that was ahead of its time. Many a tired nightshift worker of the 1970s did the 'Wellworthy Shuffle' on their way to the 7.30am ferry from Lymington. **World Ship Society**

Cenred
(1973) Wightlink
756 passengers, 76 cars
761grt; 197ft 10in (60.23m) loa
x 51ft 6in (15.68m) beam
Robb Caledon, Dundee
2 x oil, 4SA 6-cyl, by Mirrlees
Blackstone, Stamford, driving
twin Voith-Schneider
propulsion units: 1,680bhp

The *Cenred*, a sister of the
Cenwulf and the *Caedmon*, was
originally ordered for British
Rail Sealink's Lymington–
Yarmouth route but when first in
service she could be switched to
the Portsmouth–Fishbourne
passage as and when required.
She survived the corporate
transitions through Sealink UK
to the privatised Sealink British
Ferries before passing to
Wightlink in 1990. Her
operational career on The Solent
is due to be terminated in 2009
following the entry into service
on the route of newly designed
Croatian ferries. This spectacular
picture, taken on 25 October
1992, shows the *Cenred*
approaching Yarmouth on the
Isle of Wight during a fierce
gale. Even the semi-sheltered
waters of The Solent can
become rough and turbulent in
stormy conditions, especially
when crossing the shallower
waters of the bar outside
Yarmouth harbour. *Colin Elvers*

Caesarea

(11/1960) British Rail Sealink

1,400 passengers (110 sleeping berths)

4,174grt; 322ft (98.15m) loa x 53ft 8in (16.4m) beam

J. Samuel White & Company, Cowes

2 x Pametrada steam turbines, by builder, DR geared to twin screws: 9,000shp

When the *Caesarea* was launched, on 29 January 1960, she became, together with her sister the *Sarnia*, one of the two largest vessels ever built for British Railways' Channel Islands service. They were also the largest ships which could be handled in St Helier at that time. They replaced five older cross-Channel ferries. To improve passenger comfort, the *Caesarea* and *Sarnia* were fitted with anti-roll stabilisers and they offered their one-class passengers more sheltered seating for daylight trips. For night crossings there was cabin accommodation in 110 berths. Despite increased demand for vehicular traffic to the islands, the *Caesarea* was not drastically altered in any way and she coped without stern ramp modification. Her original configuration limited her sphere of operations and apart from relief duties on routes like the Dover–Calais run, she rarely departed from the route for

which she had been built until 1976, when she replaced the *Maid of Orleans*, sailing between Dover or Folkestone and Calais and Boulogne. By 1979, she had become the last purpose-built cross-Channel turbine mail/passenger steamer remaining in service. She completed that summer season with an excursion to Boulogne on 30 September for 1,128 passengers! Sold in 1980, she transferred between a number of Far East owners under the name *Aesarea*, but she never, as far as is known, undertook commercial service for any of them. She was finally scrapped in Korea, arriving there in June 1986. This view of the *Caesarea*, taken in September 1973 while alongside in Weymouth harbour, shows her long main superstructure and low fore and after decks designed to cope with all Channel conditions. *Phil Fricker*

53

Sarnia
(6/1961) British Rail Sealink
1,400 passengers (110 sleeping berths)
4,174grt; 322ft (98.14m) loa x 52ft 7in (16.03m)
beam
J. Samuel White, Cowes, Isle of Wight
2 x Pametrada steam turbines, by builder, DR geared
to twin screws; 9,000shp

Styled after the earlier *Normannia*, the *Sarnia*, photographed at St Peter Port in the summer of 1976, and her sister *Caesarea* (previous page) were ordered by the British Transport Commission to upgrade the passenger ferry service between Weymouth and the Channel Islands. Indeed, they were the largest and best-appointed railway ferries ever built for this route, exploiting a boom in holiday traffic to Jersey and Guernsey. They could be recognised by the prominent raised and tapering bulwark at the bow which was intended to give some protection to the foredeck in heavy seas. This, and the irregular line of the hull painting, did not make them the most attractive of ships. But what they may have lacked externally was more than compensated for by their interiors which brought a new standard of comfort for passengers in a single class. They had bow rudders to assist when manoeuvring astern and they were fitted with anti-roll stabilisers. The *Sarnia* continued on the Channel Islands run for the next 15 years, apart from occasional relief duties on other routes, but she did not form part of the reorganisation into Sealink UK that was to take place in 1978. After finishing on the Weymouth run in 1977, she was sold to become a floating duty-free supermarket named *Aquamart* operating from Ostend, a short-lived venture. Subsequently, she transferred to Greek owners in 1979 as the *Golden Star*, two years later moving to Saudi Arabia to become the pilgrim ship *Saudi Golden Star*, sailing between Jeddah, Aqaba and Port Said. She was broken up in Pakistan from early 1987.
Richard de Kerbrech

Condor 4

(1974) Condor Ltd,
Guernsey
136 passengers
129grt; 94ft 1in (28.68m)
loa x 35ft 2in (10.72m)
beam across foils
Cantieri Navaltecnica,
Messina
2 x Vee oil, 4SA 12-cyl, by
MTU, Friedrichshafen:
2,700bhp

Condor Ltd of Guernsey had started its hydrofoil service in 1964 with *Condor I* to provide a 'fast and exciting service' between Jersey, Guernsey and St Malo in France. Ten years after the route was inaugurated, the fourth HYD Rodriquez RHS 140 came into service, followed in 1976 by *Condor 5*. Although the route is relatively sheltered along the Cotentin peninsula, there are extreme tidal variations and strong currents off the Channel Islands. The service was seasonal and the craft were not operated between New Year and mid-March. *Condor 4* had a service speed of 32.5 knots and was capable of making the St Malo–Jersey run in 1 hour 10 minutes and, after the inter-island link, making the return run Guernsey–St Malo in 1 hour 35 minutes. By 1989, the service was carrying 430,000 passengers annually. Her hull construction was of aluminium alloy and the lift provided by Vee-style foils. *Condor 4* was withdrawn in 1993, superseded by *Condor 8*, a catamaran, and later still by wavepiercers which now also undertake crossings to and from Weymouth and Poole. She was sold to Greek interests for inter-island service as the *Iptamenos Hermes I*.

The photograph captures 'that Condor moment', as the *Condor 4* at full speed overhauls the ship from which the photographer has snapped her. **Ray Sprake**

Torpoint Ferry

Cornwall County Council and
Plymouth City Council Joint
Committee

200 passengers plus 26–28 cars

Ferry 1 & Ferry 2
(1960):
900fld; 150ft (45.71m) loa x 54ft
(16.46m) beam
John I. Thornycroft,
Southampton

Ferry 3
(1968):
940fld; 105ft (32.00m) loa x 57ft
(17.37m) beam
Charles Hill, Bristol
Diesel-electric, comprising Deutz
V8 oil engines connected to
electric motors, driving two chain
cog-wheels; bhp not known

Probably the simplest of all ferries are the 'floating
bridges' or 'chain ferries' of the type that have been
employed at various river crossings around the
country, particularly where a strong tidal flow suits a
tethered link. They have been used on the River
Orwell in Suffolk, at Southampton on the Itchen, at
Cowes (Isle of Wight) on the Medina, at Sandbanks,
Poole, and on the River Clyde between Renfrew and
Yoker, as well as at Torpoint, and many still exist.
Exploiting the operating principles of a design
conceived back in the early 1800s by James Meadows
Rendel, they have a central buoyant pontoon with
powered toothed wheels on either side positioned at
water level so that the craft can be pulled along chains
or cables that are secured on either bank and tensioned
by counterweights. Drawbridges or hydraulic prows at
each end allow the craft to use an inclined slipway for
embarkation and disembarkation. The central deck
area, given over to vehicular traffic, is flanked along
either side by enclosed passenger cabins. Built for the

crossing of the Tamar across the 2,750-foot wide
Hamoaze as it is known, were the *Lynher*, *Tamar*
and *Plym*, one of which is shown here, although it
is not certain precisely which of the three it is.
Completed with a capacity for 26–28 cars, they
were reconstructed at Falmouth during 1986–7.
This increased their individual capacity to 50–54 cars,
giving a total hourly capacity of 300 cars. It was
around this time that they were given names; they
were previously known simply as Ferry 1, Ferry 2 and
Ferry 3. Their diesel-electric engines were later
converted to diesel-hydraulic. Having had their useful
lives extended until early in the 21st century, by then
their retention was no longer viable as they were
becoming increasingly difficult and expensive to
maintain. Thus, replacement craft were procured
which took over from late in 2005, while
simultaneously the old craft were towed to
Scandinavia where they were broken up for scrap.

Cyberheritage

Northern Belle
(1927) ex *Armadillo*
(1947) Millbrook
Steamboat & Trading
Company
174 passengers
25grt; 66ft (20.11m) beam
dimensions unknown
Rogers Boatyard, Cremyll,
Cornwall
Oil: bhp not known

The ferry across the entrance to the River Tamar, linking the Cremyll peninsula with Admiral's Hard in Plymouth's Stonehouse area, was maintained privately by the Mount Edgcumbe Estate with nine small ferries until 1947 when ownership transferred to the Millbrook Steamboat & Trading Company. Among the fleet running the service at that time were two small steam-powered vessels, the *Armadillo* and *Shuttlecock*. Between 1945 and 1947, these craft were converted by their owners to diesel propulsion. They were also extensively reconstructed at the Mashfords Shipyard, the *Shuttlecock* returning to service in 1946 as the *Southern Belle* and the *Armadillo* re-emerging two years later as the *Northern Belle*.
A further change of ownership came in 1980 when the directors of Millbrook sold their shares to Dart Pleasure Craft. Five years later Dart Pleasure Craft pulled out of

the Plymouth area taking five of its vessels with it. The *Southern Belle* and *Northern Belle* were not among them, the former sold to Plymouth Boat Cruises while the *Northern Belle* was transferred to the Tamar Cruising & Cremyll Ferry Company which had taken over the ferry service. Still active, having clocked up an incredible 80 years by 2006, the *Northern Belle* now operates as an excursion vessel in Plymouth harbour and to the nearby River Yealm. She is listed in the National Register of Historic Vessels. It is thought that this undated view was taken from the jetty at Cremyll Quay, looking towards Plymouth with the Admiralty buildings at Devil's Point in the background to the right. Unfortunately, the *Northern Belle's* elegant schooner stern cannot be seen from this angle. ***Phil Fricker***

57

Devonia

(3/1956) ex *Scillonian* (1977)

P. & A. Campbell Ltd

600 passengers

921grt; 209ft 7in (63.88m) loa
x 32ft 10in (10.01m) beam

John I. Thornycroft Ltd,
Southampton

2 x oil, 4 SA 6-cyl, by Ruston
& Hornsby, Lincoln, driving
twin screws: 1,440bhp

The *Devonia* was originally built in 1956 for the Isles of Scilly Steamship Company as the *Scillonian* for service between the Isles of Scilly and Penzance. Her innovative Thornycroft funnel cowl was a novel feature adopted three years later on Red Funnel's *Carisbrooke Castle*. Not only did the *Scillonian* operate as a passenger ferry but she also carried general cargo, perishable goods and mail to the Isles of Scilly all year round and in all sea states. In 1977, the *Scillonian* was replaced by a larger ship on the route, by which time the islands also had a regular helicopter service. She was sold to P. & A. Campbell and renamed *Devonia*, for use on the Bristol Channel along with the *Balmoral*. By 1979, the new owners had decided to discontinue operations in the Bristol Channel and in 1981, the *Devonia* was put up for sale, for £100,000 (in recognition of her all-weather capability), and she was acquired in 1982, renamed *Devonium*. Further sales and renamings took place: *Syllingar* in 1984, and *Remvi*, *Africa Queen* and *Princess Eliana* in 1986. The *Devonia* was photographed in the Thames Estuary during August 1977 from the deck of the liner *Britanis*. Although this was her first season of operation on the Thames, having been transferred there briefly, strictly speaking her passenger certificate restricted her to Bristol Channel service, the limit being between Hartland Point and Milford Haven!

Richard de Kerbrech

Bristol Queen

(9/1946) P. & A. Campbell Ltd

1,197 passengers

848grt; 258ft 5in (78.7m) loa x 31ft (9.5m) beam, 59ft 9in (18.21m) across paddle sponsons

Charles Hill & Sons, Bristol

Triple-expansion 3-cyl diagonal steam reciprocating engines, by Rankin & Blackmore, Greenock, driving paddles: 2,700ihp

The *Bristol Queen* was built as a slightly larger sister to the *Cardiff Queen* in an era when steam reciprocating paddle vessels were on the wane. She was capable of a speed of 16.5 knots. Launched on 30 June 1946, she was built with hull subdivision that allowed her use on cross-Channel excursions, although none were ever undertaken. She was the first paddle steamer to be built in Bristol since 1854 and the largest owned by P. & A. Campbell. She operated on excursions in the Bristol Channel, out of Ilfracombe and Minehead, with frequent visits to the Isles of Scilly. Briefly laid up in 1959 and 1960, she returned to service in 1961. However, rising costs, declining excursion traffic and damage to a paddle wheel conspired to hasten her premature demise and, after

only 20 years in service, she was put up for disposal in 1966. Following a collision at Cardiff on 14 January 1968, she was towed to Willebroek that March to be broken up. Right to the end of her career she retained an open bridge. The photograph shows the *Bristol Queen* on 17 June 1967, steaming away from her berth at Cardiff.

World Ship Society

Cardiff Queen

(6/1947) P. & A. Campbell Ltd

1,107 passengers

765grt; 247ft 6in (75.44m) loa x 30ft (9.1m) beam, 59ft 9in (18.21m) across paddle sponsons

Fairfield, Govan, Glasgow

Triple-expansion 3-cyl diagonal steam reciprocating engines, by builder, driving paddles: 2,200ihp

P. & A. Campbell was so pleased with the performance and quality of the *Bristol Queen* that it returned to Charles Hill for a sister ship. However, at the time the Hill yard had a full order book so the order was put out to tender. The result was that Fairfield of Govan was awarded the contract to build the *Bristol Queen's* consort and she was launched on 25 February 1947. She could be distinguished from her larger sister by her teak bridge surround. She was the last paddle steamer to be built for the company and operated in consort with the *Bristol Queen* on Bristol Channel excursions. As the 1960s approached, demand for this type of day trip began to wane and she was withdrawn in 1966,

barely 20 years after first entering service. She arrived at Newport, Gwent, on 9 April 1968 for scrapping and was broken up on the River Usk. The photograph shows a fine study of the *Cardiff Queen* in her heyday, probably in the Bristol Channel, paddling along at speed.

Richard de Kerbrech collection

Balmoral

P. & A. Campbell, other details as page 43

The *Balmoral* initially joined another former Red Funnel vessel, the *Westward Ho* ex *Vecta*, on charter to Bristol-based P. & A. Campbell in 1969 and during 1969/70, she was refitted at Cosens of Weymouth and slipped at Husbands Shipyard at Marchwood. During this she was painted in P. & A. Campbell's livery and a cowl top was fitted to her funnel. P. & A. Campbell purchased her outright in 1978. She operated on many charters including some for the Paddle Steamer Preservation Society and the Coastal Cruising Association, and her various excursions took her to the South Coast, the Bristol Channel and to North Wales and Liverpool. In 1979, rising costs forced P. & A. Campbell to withdraw her from service. The *Balmoral* was briefly owned by White Funnel Steamers Ltd in 1980, by Craig Inns for intended use as a pub in 1982, and from 1986 she has operated under the ownership of Waverley Excursions Ltd following a refit. Her former car deck was later built up and decked over to form a restaurant and at the time of writing she continues to operate out of Bristol. Built in 1949, she is an example of a ferry that made the transition to the excursion vessel role, but not without financial and operational difficulties. This photograph shows the *Balmoral* in October 1974 in full P. & A. Campbell livery, leaving Swansea. *Mick Lindsay*

St Tudno

(5/1926) Liverpool & North Wales Steamship Company
2,500 passengers
2,326grt; 329ft (100.27m) loa x 44ft (13.41m) beam
Fairfield, Govan, Glasgow
4 x steam turbines, by builder, SR geared to twin screws: ship not known

One of a pair, with the similar *St Seiriol* completed five years later, which operated pleasure cruises along the North Wales coast from Liverpool to Prestatyn, Rhyl, Colwyn Bay, Llandudno and Anglesey via the Menai Strait, the *St Tudno* replaced the magnificent paddle steamer *La Marguerite* which was retired in 1925, making her maiden cruise on 22 May 1926. Built with accommodation in two classes, the *St Tudno* became a one-class ship from 1947 after she returned from war service as an Admiralty boarding vessel and a depot ship stationed at The Nore. This photograph, taken in 1955, shows her alongside one of the Menai piers. When the Liverpool & North Wales Steamship Company went into voluntary liquidation in the winter of 1962/3, it more or less brought the curtain down on a long tradition of seasonal pleasure sailings in this region. The *St Seiriol* and *St Tudno* were sold for breaking up at Ghent in Belgium, the former in November 1962, the latter in April 1963. *Kenneth Wightman*

St Trillo

(4/1936) ex *St Silio* (1945).

P. & A. Campbell Ltd

Passengers: numbers unknown

314grt; 149ft 4in (45.51m) lbp x 27ft 2in (8.28m) beam

Fairfield, Govan, Glasgow

2 x oil, 2SA 6 cyl, by builder, driving twin screws: 600bhp

Launched on 24 March 1936, the addition of the smaller, twin-funnelled *St Silio* to the *St Seiriol* and *St Tudno* represented a major investment in new tonnage by their owners over a ten-year period. Her excursion career was interrupted after just three seasons. War service from late 1939 to 1946 saw the *St Silio* attached to the examination service as an auxiliary patrol ship. She was little altered during her post-war refit but she returned to service under the new name *St Trillo*. Following the end of her final trip under the Liverpool & North Wales Steamship Company flag, on 16 September 1962, she was sold to Townsend Brothers Ferries (later Townsend Car Ferries) which immediately chartered her to P. & A. Campbell, in whose colours she is seen in this photograph from August 1973. Over the next seven years she was engaged on pleasure cruises mainly in the Bristol Channel area but, ironically, she also worked on her former owners' patch, making short cruises to Llandudno. In 1969, the *St Trillo* was laid up at Barry, South Wales, where she remained inactive for much of the next six years. She was briefly renamed *Thrillo* early in 1975, only to be sold for breaking up in Ireland. She left Barry under tow bound for Dublin on 21 April 1975. *Mick Lindsay*

Following the absorption of Coast Lines into Lord Kylsant's Royal Mail Group in 1917, a series of distinctive passenger motorships was constructed for the various Coast Lines ferry-operating subsidiaries, commencing with the *Ulster Monarch* of 1929 and two sisters for the Belfast Steamship Company. Twin-funnelled and looking like miniature versions of the White Star liners *Britannic* and *Georgic*, they were followed by four considerably more elegant single-funnelled ships, of which two, the *Royal Scotsman* and *Royal Ulsterman*, entered Burns & Laird's Glasgow–Belfast night service. This service was interrupted from the spring of 1940 and the next six years were spent as commissioned naval vessels, part of the time supporting amphibious landings as infantry landing ships. Released to their owners post-war and fully reconditioned, the pair resumed their commercial ferry duties, maintaining regular schedules for the next 20 years. Unusually, the *Royal Scotsman* is seen here berthed in Southampton's Eastern Docks in November 1967 where it is believed she may have been acting as an accommodation ship after her ferry career had ended. Briefly renamed *Royal Scotman*, two years later she became the *Apollo* under Panamanian registry. In 1984, she was again renamed but as the *Arctic Star* she survived only until May that year when she was sent to the breakers yard at Brownsville, Texas. **Kenneth Wightman**

Royal Scotsman

(5/1936) Burns & Laird Lines
550 first- and 650 second-class passengers, 30 cars
3,288grt; 339ft 8in (103.52m) loa x 47ft 8in (14.52m) beam
Harland & Wolff, Belfast
2 x oil, 2SA 8-cyl, by builder, driving twin screws: 10,400bhp

Munster

(1/1948) British & Irish Shipping Company
700 first- and 800 second-class passengers
4,142grt; 374ft 10in (114.24m) loa x 50ft 2in (15.29m) beam
Harland & Wolff, Belfast
2 x oil, 2SA 10-cyl, by builder, driving twin screws: 5,600bhp

Constructed for the British & Irish Shipping Company after World War 2 to commemorate her namesake lost to a mine on 7 February 1940 while bound for Liverpool from Belfast, the *Munster* followed the style of her predecessor and was typical of other motor passenger vessels of Coast Lines' subsidiaries operating across the Irish Sea. A sister *Leinster* replaced a ship of the same name that had been allocated to the Belfast Steamship Company in 1946 as the *Ulster Prince*. The *Munster* and *Leinster*, along with the smaller *Innisfallen*, maintained passenger services between Dublin and Liverpool, and Cork and Fishguard. A refit in 1965 gave the *Munster* a limited capacity for 25 cars. Three years later she was briefly renamed *Munster I* prior to disposal for continued service as the Mediterranean cruise ship *Theseus* of Epirotiki Lines. The following year she was transferred again, to Royal Olympic Cruises, and renamed *Orpheus*. After a long second career in this role, she was broken up at Alang where she arrived for demolition on 28 December

2000. In this view of the *Munster* berthed at Liverpool's pier head, she is seen painted in her owners' distinctive green colour scheme. **Kenneth Wightman**

Lady Killarney
(3/1912) ex *Patriotic*
(1930) ex *Lady Leinster*
(1938) ex *Lady
Connaught* (1947),
Coast Lines Ltd

200 passengers

3,222grt; 325ft 4in
(99.18m) loa x 41ft 7in
(12.70m) beam

Harland & Wolff, Belfast

Triple-expansion 8-cyl
steam reciprocating, by
builder, driving twin
screws: ihp not known

Seen berthed alongside the Princes Landing Stage, Liverpool, her straight stem and counter stern revealing her age, the *Lady Killarney* was at this time nearing the end of her working life. Originally built as *Patriotic*, one of three sisters for the Belfast Steamship Company, the others being the *Graphic* and *Heroic*, she operated the scheduled-service ferry route to Liverpool from Northern Ireland. In 1930, she underwent an extensive refit resulting in the addition of a second funnel. At the same time, she was transferred internally, so to speak, to another Coast Lines Group concern, the British & Irish Shipping Company, to work the Dublin–Liverpool route. Prior to World War 2, she was renamed for a second time. She continued commercial service after the outbreak of war but this came to an abrupt end on 26 December 1940 when she struck a mine and was extensively damaged. Though she was declared a constructive total loss,

repairs were undertaken lasting almost three years, during which she was once again reduced to a single funnel. She was then deployed as a hospital carrier for the Normandy landings, continuing in that role to the end of hostilities. Released to her owners on 2 January 1946, a further major overhaul ensued, following which post-war service primarily took the form of seasonal excursions, an itinerary of coastal cruises to the Western Isles being offered under the banner of the parent company. She adopted Coast Lines colours from 1952, as depicted here. The *Lady Killarney* was broken up at Port Glasgow where she arrived for demolition on 17 December 1956, ending a career that had lasted for 44 years. It is interesting to note that her completion in March 1912 occurred just days before the *Titanic* was completed by the same builder. **Kenneth Wightman**

It is difficult positively to identify this pre-war Mersey ferry seen bound for Birkenhead in the late 1950s. Undoubtedly, in her red and black livery, she is a unit of the Birkenhead Corporation fleet and it is thought that she is the *Hinderton*. A larger version of the *Upton*, which later operated on The Solent for Red Funnel, the *Hinderton* along with three others of this class, the *Claughton*, *Thurstaston* and *Bidston*, completed between 1930 and 1933, were more than 100 gross tons larger and almost 10 feet (3 metres) broader in the beam. Drawing on the design of the Wallasey Corporation's *Rose* and *Lily* of 1900, with a raised upper deck that extended for almost the entire length of the hull, they maintained the broad dimensions and general layout of the typical screw-driven Mersey ferry of which this pair were the prototypes. The introduction of these ferries contributed to a change of some significance for transport across the Mersey, as the paddle-driven vessels of the previous generation were progressively replaced by ferries with twin-screw propulsion. The *Hinderton* survived until September 1958 (withdrawn from service and laid up on May 1956) when she was broken up at Boom in Belgium. Note the radial lifeboat davits right at the stern and her distinctive timber bridge and bridge wings. **Kenneth Wightman**

Hinderton
(12/1925) Birkenhead Corporation
1,430 passengers
484grt; 158ft 6in (48.30m) loa x 42ft 7in (12.98m) beam
Cammell Laird, Birkenhead
2 x triple-expansion 4-cyl steam-reciprocating, by builder, driving twin screws:
ihp not known

Mountwood
(1/1960) Merseyside
Passenger Transport
Executive
1,200 passengers
464grt; 152ft 3in (46.40m)
loa x 39ft (11.90m)
beam
Philip & Son, Dartmouth
2 x oil 8-cyl, by Crossley
Brothers, Manchester;
1,360bhp

Completed to the account of Birkenhead Corporation and launched on 31 July 1959, the *Mountwood* and her sisters *Woodchurch* and *Overchurch* were designed by the Liverpool naval architects Graham & Woolnough, drawing on the design of their earlier Wallasey Corporation-owned counterparts *Leasowe* and *Egremont*. Working the Liverpool–Woodside service, they were popular additions to the Mersey ferry fleet, having light, modern passenger spaces. No vehicles were carried, a practice that had ended with the opening of the Mersey road tunnels. The *Mountwood* was immortalised in the film *Ferry Across the Mersey* (1965), based on the Gerry and the Pacemakers hit record of the same title. Municipal ownership of the Mersey ferries ended on 1 December 1969 when the fleets of the Birkenhead and Wallasey Corporations were merged under the control of the Merseyside Passenger Transport Executive and from that date all ferries were painted in a common livery. In this view of the *Mountwood* from 14 April 1979, her rubbing

strakes are prominent, an essential feature for vessels continually berthing at the end of regular 20-minute crossings. The *Mountwood* was renamed *Royal Iris of the Mersey* in 2002 and continues in service. **Jim McFaul**

64

Woodchurch
(5/1960) Merseyside
Passenger Transport
Executive
1,200 passengers
464grt; 152ft 3in (46.40m)
loa x 39ft (11.90m)
beam

Philip & Son, Dartmouth
2 x oil 8-cyl, by Crossley
Brothers, Manchester:
1,360bhp

Launched on 28 October 1959 and completed to the account of Birkenhead Corporation, the *Woodchurch*, sister to the *Mountwood*, is seen in a photograph taken on 28 June 1970, painted in cream and black livery, one of several colour schemes adopted by the Merseyside Passenger Transport Executive. After more than 20 years of regular service, from the early 1980s the *Woodchurch* and her Mersey ferry consorts entered a period of uncertainty as to their future, characterised by long periods of lay-up. The increased use of the Mersey tunnels, as the migration to private car ownership continued to escalate, had resulted in a major decline in passenger numbers and revenues. Continuation of the ferry operation was put seriously in doubt but in response to popular demand to retain this iconic service, intrinsically linked with the city's heritage, the *Woodchurch* and her consorts were extensively refurbished from 1989 and returned to full operation by July 1990. The cruise ships that, by then, were beginning to visit the port more frequently gave them a new lease of life, extending their range of employment in the form of ship-to-shore tender work and sightseeing cruises. The *Woodchurch* was renamed *Snowdrop* in 2004, reviving another link with the Mersey ferries of the past, and she remains in service under that name. **Jim McFaul**

65

Overchurch (2/1962) Merseyside
Passenger Transport
Executive
1,200 passengers
468grt; 152ft 7in (46.50m) loa
x 39ft (11.90m) beam
Cammell Laird, Birkenhead
2 x oil 8-cyl, by Crossley
Brothers, Manchester;
1,360bhp

Though similar to fleetmates *Mountwood* and
Woodchurch, unlike that pair the *Overchurch* was
constructed locally at Birkenhead, unlike that pair the *Overchurch* was
Cammell Laird shipyard on 24 November 1961, and
was the first all-welded Mersey ferry. A feature of these
ferries was that they had a central wheelhouse and two
detached, enclosed bridge wings instead of a flying
bridge (see the *Mountwood* on page 64). However,
during subsequent refurbishments, the gaps between the
wings and the wheelhouse on all three vessels were
plated-in to provide a continuous, beam-wide bridge

structure as shown here. When this photograph was
taken on 11 August 1998, the *Overchurch*, looking
smart and freshly painted, was acting as a passenger
tender and tour craft for the visiting cruise ship *Legend
of the Seas*. In the background the familiar Liverpool
city skyline can be seen, with the 'Three Graces' on the
pier head (the Liver Building, the former Cunard White
Star building and the Mersey Docks & Harbour Board
building) standing out prominently. A year after this
picture was taken the *Overchurch* was re-engined and
renamed *Royal Daffodil* (see next page). *Jim McFaul*

Royal Daffodil
(2/1962) ex *Overchurch* (1999),
Merseyside Passenger Transport
Executive
860 passengers
468grt; 152ft 7in (46.50m) loa x
39ft (11.90m) beam
Cammell Laird, Birkenhead
2 x CW6L170 oil by Wärtsilä
NSD UK Ltd: ca. 1,870bhp

In this view of the former *Overchurch* under the new name *Royal Daffodil*, and still looking absolutely pristine, she is seen arriving at the Birkenhead terminus on 13 October 1999. At the time that she and her two fleetmates were renamed, *Royal Daffodil* was adopted as the name for the *Overchurch* as it had long and special associations with the River Mersey, recalling the brave duties performed by two of these little ferries in World War 1. They were the Wallasey Corporation-owned *Iris II* and *Daffodil* which took part in the raid on Zeebrugge on 23 April 1918. In recognition of their participation in what was a dangerous naval operation, they were granted the prefix 'Royal', thereafter becoming respectively the *Royal Iris II* and *Royal Daffodil*. The *Royal Daffodil* ex *Overchurch* remains in service as a continuing reminder of that proud heritage.
Jim McFaul

Tynwald
(8/1947) Isle of Man
Steam Packet Company
2,288 passengers
2,493grt; 345ft (105.15m)
loa x 47ft (14.32m)
beam
Cammell Laird,
Birkenhead
4 x steam turbines, by
builder, SR geared to
twin screws; 8,500shp

One of six similar vessels, introduced on the Isle of Man services to replace war losses, the *Tynwald* was third of the group to enter service. The others were the *King Orry* in April 1946, *Mona's Queen* in June 1946, *Snaefell* in July 1948 (see next page), *Mona's Isle* in March 1951 and *Manxman* in May 1955, all in all an intensive building programme by any standard, besides being a highly lucrative order for Cammell Laird. Little was it appreciated at the time, but they were to be the last all-passenger ferries built for the company, the revolution in private car ownership along with the trend for touring holidays leading to the introduction of RoRo car ferries as their replacements. Nevertheless, these six ships gave

sterling service for over a quarter of a century, later refits increasing their passenger numbers and providing a modicum of car space. The *Tynwald* commemorated a similar-sized Isle of Man Steam Packet Company passenger ferry built in 1937 by Vickers-Armstrongs at Barrow and lost off Bougie, North Africa, on 12 November 1942, sunk by bombs and torpedoes. In this view of the *Tynwald* at Liverpool on 4 September 1965, she looks in need of a spruce-up. Ten years later she was disposed of for scrap, arriving at Avilés, Spain, on 10 February 1975 for demolition to commence.
Richard de Kerbrech collection

Snaefell

(7/1948) Isle of Man Steam Packet
Company
2,245 passengers
2,489grt; 345ft (105.15m) loa x
47ft (14.32m) beam
Cammell Laird, Birkenhead
4 x steam turbines, by builder, SR
geared to twin screws: 8,500shp

Fourth of her class to enter service, besides her year-round scheduled sailings on the Liverpool–Douglas route, the *Snaefell* along with the company's other ships also operated summer passenger services to and from Ardrossan, Heysham, Llandudno, Belfast and Dublin. It is an indication of the boom in holiday traffic to the Isle of Man during the 1950s that the route supported the six vessels of this class, besides other surviving pre-war ships. During a refit in the 1960s, the *Snaefell*'s passenger capacity was increased to 2,351 and she was also given space for 70 cars, responding to the growing vogue for motor-touring holidays. Photographed here between voyages, at Liverpool's Princes Landing Stage in July 1967, the *Snaefell* was broken up for scrap at Blyth, from 8 September 1978. ***Kenneth Wightman***

70

Naom Éanna
(4/1958) Córas Iompair Éireann
312 passengers
483grt; 137ft 3in (41.83m) loa
x 27ft 11in (8.51m) beam
Liffey Dockyard Company,
Dublin
Oil, 2SA 6-cyl, by British Polar
Engines, Glasgow, driving a
single screw; 630bhp

Photographed in June 1967 at Galway, as evidenced by
the McDonogh fertilizer warehouses in the
background, the *Naom Éanna* was an unusual small
passenger ferry, constructed for her owner's service
from Galway to the Aran Islands, off Ireland's west
coast. Between May and September of each year she
also regularly plied between Galway, Limerick and
Westport. She was launched on 26 October 1957,
entering service seven months later. After 30 years
maintaining the operation conveying supplies to this
remote offshore community, she was withdrawn from

service in November 1988. Then, after she failed an
inclining test for the Irish Department of the Marine,
her passenger ship safety certificate was not renewed.
Fortunately, the Irish Nautical Trust intervened to
rescue her from a likely fate of demolition for scrap.
Under the name *Naomh Éanna*, she was transferred to
Charlotte Quay in the Grand Canal Dock Basin at
Dublin where she is now leased to the Flagship Scuba
and Surfdock as a diving centre, while she also acts as
the Irish Nautical Trust's headquarters. *Ray Sprake*

Duke of Lancaster
(8/1956) British Railways Board
1,800 passengers
4,797grt; 376ft 1in (114.64m) loa x 57ft 4in (17.48m) beam
Harland & Wolff, Belfast
2 x steam turbines, by builder, DR geared to twin screws: 10,500shp

The *Duke of Lancaster* was launched on 1 December 1955 and was the first of a trio of railway steamers built for the London Midland Region for service on the Heysham–Belfast run. She ran in consort with the *Duke of Argyll* and *Duke of Rothesay* on this route, all three fitted with fin stabilisers and originally catering for 600 first-class and 1,200 second-class passengers. The *Duke of Lancaster* and her sisters were also designed for summer cruising with limited accommodation to Denmark, Belgium, France and the Netherlands. In 1979, she was renamed the *Duke of Llanerch-y-Mor* after a small hamlet in Flintshire on the coast of the Dee Estuary. The *Duke of Lancaster* is photographed here in her original British Railways livery in the unusual setting of Southampton Docks. As the picture is undated, but pre-1963, one can only speculate that, judging by her pristine paintwork, she has been recently refitted and dry-docked at Southampton. Alternatively she could be relieving either the *Falaise* or *Normannia* while they were undergoing their annual refit. ***Sail & Steam***

Duke of Lancaster
British Rail Sealink
4,450grt
All other details as previous picture

Another view of the *Duke of Lancaster*, this time sporting her Sealink livery, alongside at Holyhead. When withdrawn from service in 1987 she was towed to a creek at Mostyn on the Dee Estuary, near the village of Llanerch-y-Mor, after which she had been renamed, and beached there. Plans to use her as an exhibition centre or floating nightclub failed to come to fruition, perhaps not surprisingly given that the location was rather 'off the beaten track', and at the time of writing she remains in her virtually land-locked berth. No doubt, she will most likely have to be broken up as she lies, an ignominious end for a relic of the days of turbine steamers and overnight sleeper and mail services. Nostalgia is not what it used to be and this will give way to reality when the asbestos lagging from her turbines has to be dealt with.
Phil Fricker

King George V
(9/1926) David MacBrayne
Ltd
814 passengers
985grt; 270ft 3in (82.37m) loa
x 32ft 1in (9.78m) beam
William Denny & Bros,
Dumbarton
6 x steam turbines, by Parsons
Marine Turbine Company,
Wallsend-on-Tyne, SR
geared to twin screws:
3,000shp

The *King George V* provided much needed work for the employees of William Denny's Dumbarton shipyard during lean times. She was launched on 29 April 1926 and, although built on similar lines to the twin-funnelled paddle steamers of the day, she was a turbine screw-driven vessel. She was constructed with a low, slim hull, incorporating a bow rudder and extensive glazed-in spaces for the sightseers. Above the main deck was more covered accommodation. Built for Turbine Steamers Ltd, she passed to MacBrayne control in 1935 and was placed on the cruise service from Oban to Staffa, Iona and Mull. War service involved participation at the evacuation of Dunkirk

followed by troop tender duties on the Clyde. From 1946, apart from very occasional appearances on the Ardrishaig mail run, she resumed her summer cruise operations based at Oban. By 1966, she was the only steamer remaining in a fleet of 13 vessels, but at 16 knots, the fastest. Around this time her passenger certificate was rerated, having previously been for 1,432 passengers in two classes. This close-up view of the *King George V* was taken in 1967 while she was anchored off the approaches to Iona. A local harbour launch has come alongside to board passengers for the return trip. ***Phil Fricker***

King George V

In 1973, despite her advancing years, the *King George V* remained part of the merged company of Caledonian MacBrayne and was painted in the new concern's livery, but it was only to be for a year as she was withdrawn from service in 1975 and sold to Bristol Channel Ship Repairers Ltd. In 1981, she was sold on to Bass Charrington for conversion into a floating restaurant to be located at Cardiff, to where she was towed. During the course of this, whilst in drydock at Cardiff, she caught fire on 25 August 1981 and was gutted beyond repair. Her charred hulk was laid up until 1984 when demolition commenced locally at Tiger Bay. The photograph shows the *King George V* in the drydock at Cardiff while undergoing conversion, prior to the outbreak of fire which destroyed her. There looks to be little activity going on, and the canvas tops to her funnels confirm that she has been laid up for a long period. Note the tall stovepipe with the 'H' terminal on the quarterdeck, probably serving the crew's galley. *Phil Fricker*

Lochfyne
(5/1931) David MacBrayne Ltd
1,900 passengers
754grt; 218ft 6in (66.59m) loa
x 30ft 1in (9.17m) beam
William Denny & Bros,
Dumbarton
Diesel-electric, comprising
2 x oil, 2SA 4-cyl, by British
Polar Engines, Glasgow,
connected to electric motors,
by Metropolitan Vickers,
Manchester, driving twin
screws: 1,540bhp (1,340shp)

After 42 years working primarily on the MacBrayne
mail service to Ardrishaig as well as making summer
excursions from Oban to Staffa, Iona and Mull, the
distinctive twin-funnelled diesel-electric ferry Lochfyne
was renamed Old Lochfyne in 1973 as a precursor to
her disposal. In fact, she was broken up a year later,
from 15 March 1974, at Dalmuir. She was an
interesting vessel in a number of respects, instantly
recognisable by her widely spaced twin funnels,
but was also unusual for her diesel-electric engine
arrangement, being the first British-registered vessel
to have her propellers driven by direct-coupled electric
motors powered by diesel generators. Her long years
of passenger service continued uninterrupted

throughout World War 2, the only concession to the
changed circumstances being the repainting of her hull
and funnels in Admiralty grey. Post-war, in March
1953, she underwent a comprehensive overhaul by
James Lamont & Company, Port Glasgow.
Simultaneously, her original 4-stroke 5-cylinder
Paxman diesels were replaced by new British Polar
units by John G. Kincaid & Company at Greenock.
This view, taken in 1966, shows her in the Clyde
Estuary, after leaving Rothesay. At this time the
David MacBrayne company was jointly controlled by
the British Transport Commission and Coast Lines Ltd,
prior to its amalgamation with the state-owned
Caledonian Steam Packet Company. **Phil Fricker**

Duchess of Hamilton
(6/1932) Caledonian
Steam Packet Company
Ltd, Glasgow
1,918 passengers
795grt; 262ft 3in (79.93m)
loa x 35ft (10.67m)
beam
Harland & Wolff, Govan
3 x direct drive Parsons
steam turbines, by
builder, driving triple
screws; 3,800shp

The *Duchess of Hamilton* was launched at the Govan yard of Harland & Wolff on 5 May 1932 and was rather unusual in that she was a triple-screw steamer with directly coupled steam turbines. In effect this permitted her to manoeuvre as a twin-screw ship in confined and narrow waters with the third screw being engaged to boost speed while under way. As built she was originally coal-fired but during 1956 she was converted to oil fuel. During World War 2 she operated as a troopship, mainly between Stranraer and Larne. In the 1960s, she became renowned for her comfortable interiors and sumptuous breakfasts while maintaining the regular Gourock–Campbeltown service, progressively switching to cruise duties as the older paddle steamers were paid off. After some 37 years, towards the end of her 1969 season, she developed serious turbine problems which resulted in some stripping of blades. It was felt that, because of her age, repairs were financially unviable and she was laid up at Greenock. Preservation projects, including use as a floating restaurant, failed to materialise and on 24 April 1974, she was towed to Troon for demolition. This photograph shows the *Duchess of Hamilton* alongside the pier at Inveraray on 20 August 1968 while on an excursion from Dunoon via the Kyles of Bute.
David L. Williams

Queen Mary II

(5/1933) ex *Queen Mary*
(1935) Caledonian
Steam Packet Company
1,820 passengers
1,013grt; 263ft 4in
(80.26m) loa x 37ft
(11.28m) beam
William Denny & Bros,
Dumbarton
3 x direct drive Parsons
steam turbines, by
builder, driving triple
screws: 3,800shp

The *Queen Mary II* was completed for Williamson-Buchanan Steamers Ltd with two white-coloured, black-topped funnels, and was launched with the name *Queen Mary* on 30 March 1933. At the time, the giant Cunarder No.534 was under construction at Clydebank and it was the desire of the Cunard White Star directors that she also should bear this name. As duplication of names on the British Register was not permitted, an arrangement was reached with Williamson-Buchanan whereby their new ferry would be renamed and from 1935 she became the *Queen Mary II*, releasing the name of King George V's consort for the great liner. The *Queen Mary II* was transferred to the London, Midland & Scottish Railway after World War 2 and, following nationalisation, absorbed into the fleet of the Caledonian Steam Packet Company. During a refit in 1957 at the Elderslie Dockyard (now BAe Systems, Scotstoun) she had a new oil-fired boiler installed and her two slim funnels were suppressed, replaced by a single broader one of elliptical section. Late in her career on the Clyde she was engaged to a greater extent on summer excursions

from Glasgow to the Kyles of Bute and various Clyde Estuary resorts. In this view, she is seen in July 1974 leaving Gourock, probably bound across the Clyde to Dunoon. Her funnel is painted in the colours of Caledonian MacBrayne (CalMac), adopted after the merger of the Caledonian Steam Packet Company (owned by the British Transport Commission) with David MacBrayne on 1 January 1973. In essence, the state-owned concern acquired MacBrayne's ships, routes and goodwill, but the new livery was very much that of the absorbed private company with the simple addition of a yellow circle on the sides of the funnel bearing the red Caledonian lion. Retired in 1978, the *Queen Mary II*, her name again shortened to *Queen Mary* from 1976, languished for years until she was transferred to London in 1987. Opened in 1989 as a Thames-side dining and entertainment attraction, moored alongside the Victoria Embankment between Waterloo and Charing Cross bridges, she remains there to this day, once again sporting two funnels. ***Kenneth Wightman***

Caledonia

(3/1934) ex *Caledonia*
(1939) ex HMS *Goatfell*
(1946), Caledonian
Steam Packet Company
Ltd

1,730 passengers

623grt; 230ft (70.10m) loa
x 30ft (9.2m) beam, 62ft
(18.9m) across sponsons

William Denny & Bros,
Dumbarton

Triple-expansion 3-cyl
diagonal steam
reciprocating engines,
by builder, driving
paddles: 1,800ihp

The *Caledonia* was launched on 1 February 1934 for the
London, Midland & Scottish Railway as a quasi-sister to
the same company's *Mercury*. She broke from
conventional paddle-steamer appearance in that she did
not sport the ornate paddle boxes with their integral
scrollwork. Instead, her paddles were concealed within
enclosed or streamlined paddle boxes, giving the
impression, when viewed broadside on, of a screw-
propelled vessel. She was fitted with two Navy boilers
identical to those fitted in gunboats of the day. Her
itinerary, along with her sister, was a network of Clyde
services from Gourock and Wemyss Bay, with
connections to Dunoon, Rothesay and the Kyles of Bute,
with short cruises from Largs and Millport in the summer
season. From early on during World War 2, she served as
the paddle minesweeper HMS *Goatfell*, going to the aid
of her sister when she struck a mine on 24 December
1940, though without success. In 1942, she was adapted

as an auxiliary anti-aircraft vessel. Reverting to her
original name in 1946, she resumed her Clyde service
after a refit, thereafter being engaged on virtually all the
passenger routes across the Firth, with trips to Arran and
Campbeltown added to her excursion programme. The
Caledonia was re-boilered and converted to oil burning
during 1955 and remained in continuous service from
then until withdrawn in 1969. She was bought by the Bass
Charrington Group in 1970 for preservation on the River
Thames as a pub and restaurant renamed *Old Caledonia*.
But, ravaged by fire on 27 April 1980, she was deemed
beyond economic repair and was scrapped near
Sittingbourne in Kent. Her diagonal steam engines were,
however, salvaged and are preserved at Hollycombe
House, Liphook in Hampshire. This fine photograph
shows the *Caledonia* departing Rothesay on 15 July 1965.
World Ship Society

Waverley
(6/1947) Caledonian Steam
Packet Company Ltd
1,016 passengers
693grt. 240ft (73.14m) loa
x 30ft 3in (9.20m) beam,
57ft 3in (17.45m) across
paddle sponsons
A. & J. Inglis, Pointhouse,
Glasgow

Triple-expansion diagonal steam reciprocating, by Rankin & Blackmore, Greenock, driving paddles: 2,100ihp

Completed for the London & North Eastern Railway, the *Waverley* was built as a replacement for the *Waverley* of 1899, sunk during the evacuation of Dunkirk on June 1940. She was absorbed into the nationalised railway fleet within less than a year from her entry into service and served on a variety of Clyde routes as a passenger ferry and excursion steamer for the next 35 years, under the house flag of the Caledonian Steam Packet Company and, later, of Caledonian MacBrayne. Acquired for preservation soon after the end of her Clyde career, the *Waverley* is now nationally renowned and is the only

surviving working example of the great age of paddle steamers around the British coast. Thoroughly overhauled and maintained, she remains in pristine condition, thanks to the assistance of Lottery grants as well as from being on the Core Collection list of the National Register of Historic Vessels. A long future now seems to be virtually assured thanks to the patronage of enthusiasts, nostalgic trippers and benefactors alike. She maintains a regular annual programme of pleasure cruises, working anticlockwise around Britain from her home port of Glasgow. The photograph shows her leaving Gourock back in August 1972, still wearing her Caledonian Steam Packet colours. *Mick Lindsay*

Glen Sannox

(6/1957) Caledonian
MacBrayne Ltd
1,100 passengers, 55 cars
1,269grt; 256ft 6in
(78.18m) loa x 46ft 3in
(14.10m) beam
Ailsa Shipbuilding
Company Ltd, Troon
2 x oil, 2SA 8-cyl, by
Sulzer Bros, Winterthur,
driving twin screws:
4,400bhp

During 1953–4, Caledonian placed three new passenger and car ferries on the Clyde services: the *Arran, Bute* and *Cowal*. All were fitted with side ramps and a centre 14-ton lift and could be used at all states of the tide. In 1957, they were joined by an enlarged version, the *Glen Sannox*, twice their gross tonnage and built at a cost of £468,000, for similar service on the Arran route. During the winter of 1970, she was fitted with a stern ramp for use at the linkspans installed at Ardrossan, Brodick and Fairlie, which enhanced her RoRo loading capability especially with regard to commercial vehicles. She was again refitted in 1971–2 when her crane was removed and longer side ramps fitted. At the same time her original bow rudder was replaced by a bow thruster. In 1973, Caledonian MacBrayne was created and she passed to that company and was eventually repainted in its livery. A year later she was placed on the Oban–Craignure (Mull) run but, dogged by engine troubles, her original machinery installation was replaced in 1976 by two

Norwegian 2SA 7-cyl Wichmann turbocharged diesels which each developed 2,333bhp. By 1982, she had become the oldest ship in the fleet but, despite this, she did not have the nostalgic appeal of the old steam excursion vessels. In 1986, the Caledonian MacBrayne corporate-brand lettering was painted on the sides of her hull. Three years later, surplus to requirements, she was sold to Arab interests on 24 July 1989 and renamed the *Knooz*. She was rebuilt at Panama as a pilgrim ship for service on the Red Sea, later becoming the *Nadia* (1989), *Al Marwah* (1991) and *Al Basmalah* (1994). Since 2000, she has been lying in a sunken condition in the Al-shuaiba Sea, 70 kilometres south of Jeddah, after running aground. The *Glen Sannox* was photographed in the Firth of Clyde on a dull day during May 1975. Note the lion symbol on her funnel. Back in 1964, she had been the first Caledonian Steam Packet vessel to have this motif added to her livery. *Mick Lindsay*

80

Maid of the Loch
(5/1953) Ind Coope
1,000 passengers
555grt; 208ft (63.39m) loa
x 28ft 1in (8.56m) beam,
51ft 1in (15.57m) across
paddle sponsons
A. & J. Inglis, Pointhouse,
Glasgow
Compound 2-cyl diagonal
steam reciprocating, by
Rankin & Blackmore,
Greenock, driving
paddles: 900ihp

The last paddle steamer to be built in the United
Kingdom, the *Maid of the Loch* was probably also the
very last British-built ship to have compound steam
machinery. To construct such a ship, with her employment
restricted to the summer cruise season on the confines of
Loch Lomond and given her relatively large size for such
a service, was a bold step which more than once has been
called into question. For a good while at least, though,
the *Maid of the Loch* proved to be very popular and a
good revenue earner. Constructed on the Clyde, she was
transported in sections to Balloch where she was
assembled and launched on 5 March 1953. In this view,
taken many years later at Balloch, she is seen with the
small 106 gross ton *Countess Fiona* secured along her

starboard side. This latter vessel was originally the
Countess of Breadalbane completed for the London &
North Eastern Railway in 1936 and broken up in 1999
after 17 years on Loch Lomond. In this view the
Maid of the Loch is laid up inactive from
September 1983, after making her last Caledonian Steam Packet cruise in
1980. She awaits the intentions of new, brewery owners,
with canvas covering over her funnel to keep out the
elements. In fact, she was not adapted for pub/restaurant
use, no doubt because of her land-locked location.
Instead she has remained idle, but since 1996 she has
been in the hands of Loch Lomond Steamship Company's
conservationists who are planning to return her to service
once she has been fully restored. **Phil Fricker**